Healing Your Energy

An Interactive Guidebook to
Exploring Your
Chakras and Reiki Energy

Marie King Hardman, MS, RN, LMT
Reiki Master Teacher

Disclaimer:

The information in this book is not intended as medical advice and is not a substitute

for the medical recommendations of physicians or other health-care providers.

The use of energy work or Reiki is to provide the user with complementary

choices for optimal health and healing.

Note:

Reiki attunements and symbols must be provided by a Reiki Master Teacher

in order for the student to become a Reiki Practitioner.

Order this book online at www.trafford.com
or email orders@trafford.com

Most Trafford titles are also available at major online book retailers.

Print information available on the last page.

ISBN: 978-1-4907-9469-3 (sc)
ISBN: 978-1-4907-9468-6 (e)

Trafford rev. 04/12/2019

 www.trafford.com
North America & international
toll-free: 1 888 232 4444 (USA & Canada)
fax: 812 355 4082

This book is dedicated

to
my dad,
who has transitioned
to the energy of the other side.

Acknowledgements

My many thanks to...

My clients and patients
for allowing me to practice and experiment
on them for the last twelve years.
And for believing in me.

Rick Hardman of Design Productions
for his love, inspiration, devotion, encouragement,
design sense and skill, and the front cover.

Wendy West
for painstakingly editing my first book.

Reggie Groff of Groff Film, Inc.
for the artistic photography.

Paula McKinney
my friend and massage student, for being my model.

Larry Ira Landau of Dragonfly Taijiquan
for being my male model.

Cosmotech students
for my hair, make-up and nails.

Joe Charlton of Mystyc
for my web set-up and design.

Einstein the cat and Louie the dog.

Everyone who has supported me in this journey including:
Deborah Carlton, Molly Morell, Rebecca Leeman, patrons of Pete's Café,
L.P. Leja, Ellen Chapman, and Jeff Logan.

"There are only two ways to live your life.
One is as though nothing is a miracle.
The other is as though everything is a miracle."

Albert Einstein

Contents

My Story

Growing up in the 1970's, with an electrician for a father, whenever we talked of energy it related to a kitchen appliance, outlet, or automobile. It was not until 1988 that I wandered into the world of the human energy body.

I began my bachelors degree in nursing and chose an elective course entitled "Holistic Health". I was interested in health, but did not really know what that term meant. I was intrigued and drawn to the class. Many years later I would return and teach that same course.

While studying "Holistic Health", I was introduced to alternative ways and different cultures' philosophies about healing. One day a guest speaker arrived to discuss human energy. She had wild long hair and wore a purple skirt. She seemed really "out there" - little did I know how she and that course would influence my life.

Four years later, I graduated as a nurse. Only six months after working as a registered nurse in long term care, I realized "this was not it." The medical society was narrow minded, too specialized and did not see the whole person. One year later I enrolled in a massage therapy program. This became a life-altering experience for me. I packed my black Mercury Lynx to the roof and piled everything else I owned into storage. I took ten days to drive from Maine to northern California where I spent the next nine months immersed in the energy of the west coast and bodywork.

While attending massage therapy school, I heard about a particular type of energy work. It was presented as an extra evening class for those interested. I was in a space of wanting to know more about everything, so I went. The instructor spoke of healing with energy. She said you could not hurt anyone with this energy. It flowed from her hands. She could help heal herself and others. The woman told a story of her own car accident and how the medical people were amazed she healed so quickly. I was intrigued. I wanted to learn more about anything that might help make me healthier. I signed up for a class.

The first class was held in the Reiki Master's house. Her living room was comfortable, colorful and filled with objects like stones and crystals. There were five students. The instructor made us herbal tea, and loved Chinese food. She had short, brown curly hair, was in her fifties, and possessed a wonderful, wise persona. She was a Reiki Master, the highest level. It sounded very official to me. Over the next five hours she talked about energy, chakras (energy centers in the body), disease, hand positions, and Reiki.

Reiki energy is the universal life force energy in every living thing. It is natural, safe and only helps to heal. She told us the history of Reiki and how it came to the United States. Then I received my first attunement. I learned that she could not teach me Reiki. She, as a master, could attune me to Reiki energy which is at a different frequency for increased healing. I went alone with her into the back room and sat on a stool. She asked me to close my eyes. I could feel her breath blowing on me. I became extremely hot. Within a couple of minutes, we were done. I was attuned. I knew something had happened. A shift in me had occurred. The attunement process was a sacred private ceremony.

Over the next few months, I performed Reiki on myself daily. I could feel the heat and calmness from my hands. Before my attunement, my hands were always cold. What had happened? I had no explanation. I practiced on my peers at massage school. One person described the sensation as a gentle wave over her entire body.

I had finished Reiki level I and II when I graduated from massage therapy school. I returned home to open my bodywork practice. I noticed as I was massaging my clients, they would comment on how hot my hands became. They also liked whatever I was doing at the end of the massage when my hands stopped moving. That was Reiki energy. The interesting piece for me was that I was not doing anything. I had become an open channel. The healing energy flowed through me to them. They liked the way it felt, and so did I.

Over the next four years, I became more impressed by Reiki. My life was changing, for the better. My clients were increasing in their physical and emotional health. I saw some clients make leaps and bounds in their healing. Some clients had me perform only energy work for a whole hour. I felt like the Reiki had started me on a healing course in my own life. I believe becoming attuned was one of the best decisions I ever made, and I wanted to provide others with that opportunity. Finally, after four years, I decided I was ready to become a Reiki Master Teacher so I could attune other people. In 1998, I began teaching Reiki classes.

I possessed a background in curriculum development, and had designed and taught classes in massage therapy for years. I read many books on Reiki and created my teaching packet for Reiki I and II. I feel it is important for Reiki Masters to present information about Reiki in a user-friendly form, and I can now share this guidebook with other Reiki Masters to use for teaching. This is information that I have learned in my twelve years of experiencing energy work. The material is the nuts and bolts of energy work, chakras, and the basics of Reiki level I and II.

I encourage all massage therapists and nurses to understand the human energy system. I feel all health care professionals who provide direct patient care can benefit from learning and experiencing the energy body. The medical society is only beginning to utilize and appreciate the valuable healing techniques available. Currently I practice energy work on a daily basis, either with my massage clients or my patients when I am a home care visiting nurse. The benefit is always noticeable.

I hope students and teachers find this book helpful. My goal for you is self discovery and transformation. Experiment with the exercises and ponder the results. Enjoy the journey.

In good health,

Marie

SECTION I – INTRODUCTION TO YOUR ENERGY

Chapter 1
Healing Your Energy

We are all energy beings. A wise person once said, "We are not physical beings with an energetic body, we are energetic beings in a physical body." Energy makes up every cell of our body. Our physical body is composed of billions of cells. These tiny cells use an energy process at the beginning of life to divide and produce more cells. These cells bind together to create fibers, which in turn form tissues, then muscles, organs and skin. Therefore, by the simplest definition, we are energy beings.

Whether acting in my role as a nurse or massage therapist, when I am focused on caring for your physical body, I am interacting with your energy body. Your energy field, also known as subtle energy bodies, is penetrated when a practitioner is within a few inches of your physical body. Touching another person enmeshes the energy of the two people. Health care providers who are not aware of this phenomenon may feel drained at the end of a work day. They may inadvertently give away their energy.

When we are interacting with a person's physical body, we cannot help but touch the energetic body. Whether you are a nurse, nurse assistant, massage therapist, physical therapist, or occupational therapist, you delve into your client's energy field every day. You can tell if they are angry or grieving. You can even pick up that emotion yourself if you are unaware of the power of energy.

This book is designed to help you learn about the energy of your body and how you can use it effectively to release your past and pursue the future you desire. Exercises are provided to allow you opportunities to look at your energy as not something you should ignore, but the core of what makes up every cell of your being. Every event you ever experienced in your lifetime is held in the tissues and cells of your body. Hanging onto the energy of past experiences and reliving them subconsciously every day decreases your energy potential to heal yourself and live your life to the fullest each day.

We use our energy to accomplish what we believe we want. However, when we run out of energy to finish the task, it is taken from the energy in our cell tissues. Caroline Myss discusses this topic in her video *"The Energetics of Healing"*. Weakened body cells turn into dis-ease and illness. It is important to take stock of your life to evaluate where your energy is going, and what is replenishing you. If you do not like your results, it is time for a change.

Emotions are also energy which cannot be seen. All emotions are held in the energetic body. Unresolved emotional issues, including grief, anger, fear, depression and guilt, stay in your energetic system and may over time cause physical pain, illness or dis-ease. Balancing the energy system releases and clears past and present emotional and physical disorders in the body.

Your physical, emotional and energetic bodies always move toward healing and wholeness. If you provide an environment of openness, healing will be attracted to you.

There are many ways to start healing your energy system. This book discusses ways to open your energy system so it functions at its highest level. Then stuck emotions and the past can begin to heal. Healing yourself is the first step to healing others. Your goal includes healing your energy so in turn your clients may feel your healing energy.

Your Top Ten List

Write down your top ten stressors. What in your life is draining your energy? It can be people, places, or things. The stressor may be big or small, but if it is stressing you, it counts.

1. _____

2. _____

3. _____

4. _____

5. _____

6. _____

7. _____

8. _____

9. _____

10. _____

Now beside each one, write down where you are feeling that stress in your body.

This list is affecting your physical and emotional health. What can you change or decrease on this list?

Your Energy Enhancer List

Write down your top ten favorite activities. What increases your energy? How do you like to play? What makes you happy?

1. _____

2. _____

3. _____

4. _____

5. _____

6. _____

7. _____

8. _____

9. _____

10. _____

This is your own energy enhancer list. How many activities did you engage in this week? Put a check mark beside each activity you performed this week, a second check mark if you did it at least three times this week, and a third check mark if you did it today.

How many activities have three checkmarks?   _____

Do you have at least ten check marks?   _____

Make time for yourself every day.

Feel Your Energy

Try this exercise. Place your hands, palms facing, one to two inches apart, in front of you. Rub your palms together. Now move your hands in a circle, passing fingers and palms. Do this for a minute. Then pull your hands a few inches farther apart. Imagine there is a balloon between your palms and slowly push against the balloon. Notice what you sense between your hands. There are no right or wrong feelings. You may notice sensations of tingling, pulsating, heat, or cold. How far apart can you bring your hands and still feel energy in your hands? Take your time practicing this exercise. You may close your eyes. Remember to breathe. Pay attention to the sensations. That is your energy.

We are energetic beings. Our energy affects our health. Other people's energy also affects our health. Now try this exercise. Practice with a partner sitting in a chair. Place your hands, thumbs touching and palms open and down about two feet above your partner's head. Now, close your eyes and slowly lower your hands over your partner's head. Stop your hands when you feel the energy from your partner's head. Open your eyes. How far away are your hands? When could you feel the energy? What did it feel like? What did your partner feel?

Practice feeling your or someone else's energy every day and your ability to do so will become stronger.

Try this Exercise

Write a description of what happened:

Chapter 2
Intention and Intuition

The two most powerful words to the Universe are: Intention and Intuition. By Universe, I mean whatever term responds to your psyche as a more substantial being than yourself. Other names include: Great Spirit, Higher Power, The Many, Angels, God, and Allah. Use whichever one feels right for you.

Speaking your intention puts the attention of the Universe on high alert. You have made a choice. You want to change something in your life. Be careful what you ask for, you might just get it. This statement may be more real than you realize. The Universe is paying attention. Now, what do you choose?

Your intention is a statement to the Universe that you have made a choice. I intend to create healing for my clients. My intention is to heal myself and others gently. Your intention may manifest quickly or slowly. Remember the Universe has no sense of time. What we imagine will occur in a week may take years. The Universe also has a wonderful sense of humor. Remember to be specific and clear when stating your intention. Your words will be taken literally. If you ask for passion in your relationship, it may not end up being with your current partner. Be clear.

Intentions can be used like affirmations. Affirmations are also statements about what we choose. I like to invite my clients to state their intention of the body/energy work session before they lie on the table. I have one client who states, "I have to be careful here, I know what I say will happen." She has seen the force of her words.

It is possible to manifest anything you put your mind or energy toward. Your thought is energy. Thought is followed by action. Action creates change. You can use up all of your energy until you have none left. Carolyn Myss talks about us being "energetic bankers". If we spend more than we have, the energy debt comes out of our tissue cells. Thus, people become physically sick. So choose your intention wisely.

Intuition is a knowing without knowing why or how. It is information received beyond using the normal five senses. Intuition is trust. It is the BIG trust. Trusting your intuition means you are okay. You are safe. You can stop being in control. We like being in control in America. It is the wonderful false sense of security that helps us get through the day. Feeling like we are in control provides our safety net. However, we are never really safe – only in our minds. Everything is in our minds. Our intuition is bypassing the brain and trusting our minds to lead us in the direction of healing, peace, safety. We cannot be in control and trusting our intuition at the same time, though we try. Your intuition suggests ideas which may not make sense, or have current meaning. However, if you can follow the thought through, you may find you are exactly where you choose to be. Your intuition is smarter than your brain could ever be because the information comes from the Universe – a force larger than life…an energy you cannot see, but, if you are lucky, you will hear it or feel it.

If you start to trust your intuition, even a little at first, it will become stronger. Your intuition will begin to talk to you more often. And when you forget and ignore it like a friend of mine once did, an "accident" may happen. That little voice in her head said "Tie your shoe. Tie your shoe." She chose not to, tripped, and broke her arm. She knew better. Sometimes the words are warnings: "Duck." Sometimes directions: "Turn right." Sometimes a message for healing: "Ponder the stuckness in your body." Sometimes "accidents" really are "oops's". Many times they are messages from the Universe. The Universe and your body are always trying to get your attention in order to talk to you. I was working as a nurse at a job that was draining all my energy. I was exhausted all the time. I knew I should leave the job soon. One day, as I was focused on a patient, but also rushing around, I forcefully hit my head on a wall light. I almost knocked myself out, and ended up with a concussion. Two weeks later I gave my notice. It is easier if you take time to listen instead of being hit on the head, literally.

So, learning to use your intention and listening to and trusting your intuition can be the beginning of healing your energy and yourself. If you respect your intention and intuition, you may use them to heal yourself. We all need energy vibrating at a higher level. The more each person's energy vibrates higher, the higher the earth's energy vibrates. Healing our world is our biggest challenge.

Try this Exercise

Intention Exercises

1. To practice writing affirmations as intentions, turn to Chapter 12 which describes affirmations in more detail.

2. Practice holding the intention for someone else. Practice with a partner lying down on her back. Place your right hand behind the back of her head over the base of the skull. When the person has relaxed and allowed you to hold her head, gently place your left palm over her heart (mid-sternum) area. Wait for her head and heart to connect. Focus your intention on being present for that person. Witness the release as you provide an intention of safety and acceptance.

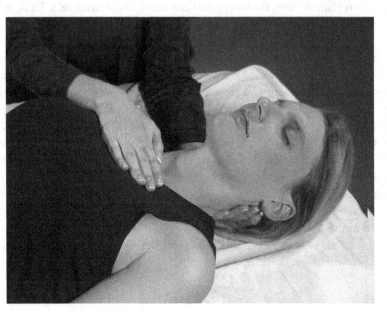

Intuition Exercises

Begin by being quiet. What thoughts come into your head? Do you listen to them? Imagine an angel sitting on your shoulder whispering into your ear. Do you hear what she says? It may be something small like, "Turn left" or "Tie your shoe". If you do what you feel you are being told, even if you have no proof of why, you might discover serendipity. The more you trust this little voice and act as if it is real, the more it will speak to you.

1. Sit across from a partner. It can be someone you know or do not know at all. One person will practice being a sender and one a receiver. Many people are better at one role or the other. Begin by having the sender and receiver close their eyes to help block out visual distractions. Then have the sender think of a color. Concentrate on that color. See it in your mind. Practice each exercise for less than 30 seconds. Let the image come into your brain. Can the receiver tell you what color you were thinking of?

2. Next try thinking of a shape, like a triangle, circle, or square. Concentrate and see if the other person can pick up your energy vibe. Imagine drawing the shape in your mind.

3. Then think of a number between one and ten. Again concentrate on only one number. Have the receiver guess your number; how close are they? Did they sense the number three when you were thinking of the number eight?

After one person has been the sender, switch and let the receiver try sending. Start back at the beginning with choosing a color. You can write down and date your responses.

4. Sit across from a partner. It might work better if you do not know the person very well. Take a deep breath and look at your partner's face. Start speaking. Say whatever pops into your head. Talk non-stop for three minutes. Do not judge yourself. Afterwards, get feedback from your partner on what you said. Then switch roles. Trusting your intuition comes from practice and from believing in yourself. Self-judgment, or a fear of "being wrong", blocks your innate ability to receive messages that the universe is sending to you, and to each one of us, every day.

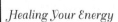

Chapter 3
Your Energy Body

Your human energy body consists of the aura, chakras and meridians. These three elements cannot be seen by most people. However, many people can become sensitive to the body's energy and feel the aura, chakras and meridians. Your aura is composed of seven layers of energy that surround your physical body. Chakras are the energy centers of the body. Balanced chakra and meridian energy help keep your organs healthy. The Chinese use the twelve meridian pathways, or energy lines, in the body to assess and treat health. In Traditional Chinese Medicine, hundreds of acupuncture points along the meridians are accessed to release Chi energy. A person who performs acupuncture or shiatsu is contacting meridian energy. Dealing with meridians is an individual specialty and will not be detailed in this book.

Your Aura

Your aura, also known as auric field, is the human energy field that envelops your body. It extends out from your physical body to beyond where your hands can reach. Your aura interacts with your chakra system, affecting your emotional and physical health. When you are carrying old emotional burdens of anger, depression, guilt, or grief, your aura may become saturated. A heavy or overwhelmed aura over time may produce emotional and physical illness or pain. It is important to clear the aura when releasing past emotions. Every time you provide direct health care to a client, you are entering his auric field. If you focus on feeling aura energy, your intuition for sensing it will improve. You can learn to feel the aura with your hands. Practice the following exercises to raise your awareness of auras.

Aura Exercises

Feeling Your Aura

Open your left palm in front of you. Place the fingertips of your right hand two inches from your left palm. Move your right hand in a clockwise circular direction. What sensations do you feel? You may close your eyes for more concentration. After one minute, switch hands. Is there a difference between your palms?

Assessing and Smoothing the Aura

Practice with a partner who is lying down on her back. Place your hands two inches above the top of her head with your palms facing toward her head.

Begin slowly sweeping your hands down the front of your partner's body, keeping them two inches above the body. Sweep using three lines, the head and middle of the body, the outer torso and legs, then the arms and outer legs to the feet. Notice the sensations you pick up from your partner's body. What areas feel hot or cold? Areas that feel different are asking for more attention and clearing. You can sweep your hands down the body as many times as you want. You are clearing the aura more with each swipe. The aura is more balanced when you do not notice areas that feel different.

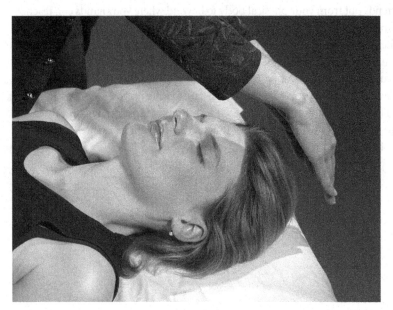

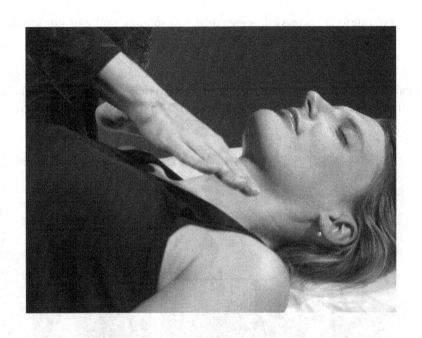

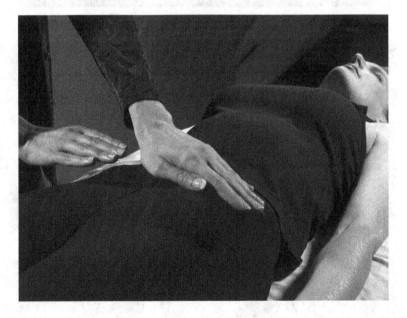

Fluffing the Aura

If you are feeling depressed, or even tired, have someone fluff your aura for a quick pick-me-up.

While your partner is standing, place your hands near her feet. Begin moving your hands, palms up, in a circular motion. Slowly move your hands up the body to the head. Fluff the front and back side of the body. Notice how you feel after you have been fluffed.

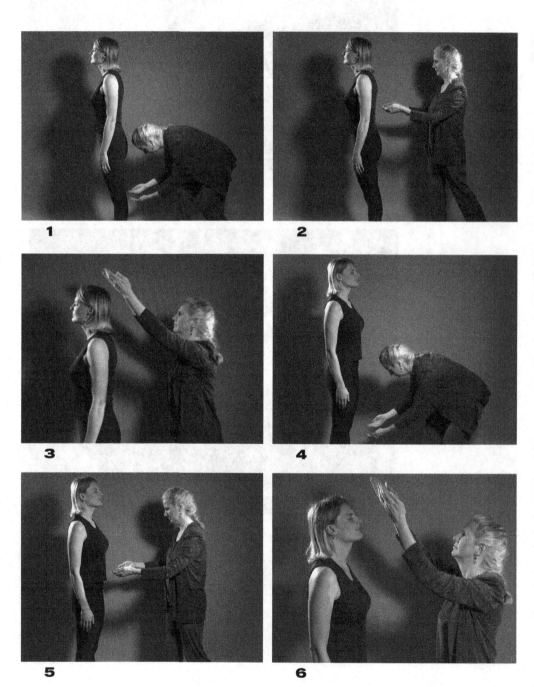

1

2

3

4

5

6

Your Chakra System

The belief in chakra energy has existed for over 5000 years. Its history is rooted in the yoga practice in India. The word chakra originates from the Sanskrit language and means wheel or disk. The chakras are spinning vortices of energy found along the spinal column or midline of the physical body. Each chakra corresponds to a different location in the body, an organ, emotion, color, sound, crystal, frequency and psychological behavior. Chakra energy connects us to the universal energy field.

There are at least seven major chakra energy centers. Four minor chakras can also be found in the palms of the hands and soles of the feet. The major chakras are an energy system. Each one responds to the others. When all chakras are balanced, they touch when spinning in a clockwise direction and are all about the same size. The lower chakras spin at a lower vibration and the upper chakras spin at a higher vibration.

Chakras hold our emotional events of the past. Donna Eden, author of *Energy Medicine* states that if she has only one session with a client, she focuses on the chakra system because she can connect to the client's history. A history of physical or emotional trauma may have caused a chakra to be blocked or closed. Blocked chakras may eventually cause physical and emotional illnesses. Chakras can be open, closed, over-active, under-active, or blocked. When all your chakras are open, a state of balance is achieved, and you are at your healthiest and whole.

Chakras spin in a clockwise or counterclockwise direction. When a chakra spins in a forward or clockwise direction, it is open to receiving universal energy. A counterclockwise spinning chakra is closed to receiving universal energy. As a direct care professional, you may spin a chakra counterclockwise to pull out toxins from the body. This is called clearing a chakra, and is taught at the end of this chapter.

Instead of using the stagnate terms open or closed, more accurate terms are over-active or under-active which provide opportunity for fluid movement of a chakra. Over-active chakras compensate for under-active chakras. Therefore, it is extra important to focus on opening an under-active chakra instead of focusing on decreasing an over-active chakra. There are many techniques to open your chakras.
The goal is to open and balance the entire chakra system.

What I tend to notice as a healthcare professional in this country is many clients have the same pattern to their chakras. It is common to see an over developed second chakra which is numbed by an addiction to food, alcohol, drugs or sex. An over active second chakra causes the first chakra to be under-active which makes sense because the person does not have the feelings of basic safety in his or her life. This also causes the third chakra to be under-active because the person displays low self-esteem. Also the fourth chakra is under-active in America where people hold on to anger and do not forgive each other or express enough love and compassion toward others. Instead the fifth chakra is over-active as we talk openly on cell phones in public and have lost our sense of boundaries and forgotten how to listen. A small majority of health care providers are opening their sixth and seventh chakras, realizing that our traditional modern medicine is greatly lacking

when caring for the whole person, and that other holistic techniques are invaluable at this time in our lives. Remember, the energy body always moves toward wholeness, so you will be attracted to an individual whose chakra system is open opposite of yours, which is why opposites attract. Learn what you can from that relationship, but know the ultimate goal in healing is balance.

Opening a chakra may take only a few minutes. However, keeping it open is more difficult. Chakras can begin to close down daily due to our current lifestyles and stress. It takes a conscious effort to become a clear energy channeler. It is important to practice clearing your chakras every day. Then you may assist others in healing at the highest energetic level.

Daily stressors affect your chakras. There are many causes for a chakra to be out of balance. Blocked chakras can occur from long-term negative experiences such as:

- ∞ Stress
- ∞ Pain
- ∞ Lack of sleep
- ∞ Poor diet
- ∞ Illness
- ∞ Grief
- ∞ Depression

List below any of these symptoms or other symptoms you may be experiencing. Notice which chakras they relate to as you answer the self-assessment questions.

_____

_____

_____

_____

_____

_____

_____

_____

_____

_____

_____

_____

_____

_____

_____

_____

_____

The Chakra System

Chakra	Name	Location	Organ	Color	Keynote
1	Root or Base	base of spine	kidneys intestines	red	C
2	Sacral	low back below navel	bladder reproductive organs	orange	D
3	Solar Plexus	above navel	stomach liver pancreas	yellow	E
4	Heart	sternum chest	heart lungs	green pink	F
5	Throat	throat	throat thyroid	bright blue	G
6	Third Eye or Brow	brow forehead	eyes ears sinus	indigo blue	A
7	Crown	top of head	brain nervous system	violet white	B

The following pages provide self-assessment questions to discover which of your chakras are unbalanced or under-active. Answer them honestly. After reviewing this chapter, write the number of checkmarks you have recorded in the "Always" column beside each chakra below to reveal your chakra system. Then, notice which chakras seem to need the most support. Focus on your under-active chakras. They will have the highest numbers. Practice the methods to open and balance your under-active chakras.

Chakra	Always
7	☐
6	☐
5	☐
4	☐
3	☐
2	☐
1	☐

The First Chakra (Your Root Chakra)

SELF-ASSESSMENT

Answer the following questions by placing a checkmark under the corresponding column.

	Never	Sometimes	Always
1. Do you feel unsafe?	☐	☐	☐
2. Do you feel insecure?	☐	☐	☐
3. Do you feel ungrounded?	☐	☐	☐
4. Does your life feel unstable?	☐	☐	☐
5. Do you feel disconnected from your physical body?	☐	☐	☐
6. Do you feel nervous?	☐	☐	☐
7. Are you fearful?	☐	☐	☐
8. Are you materialistic?	☐	☐	☐
9. Are you greedy?	☐	☐	☐
10. Do you resist change?	☐	☐	☐
11. Do you experience constipation?	☐	☐	☐
12. Do you experience frequent colds?	☐	☐	☐
13. Do you feel uneasy in your house?	☐	☐	☐
14. Do you move more than once a year?	☐	☐	☐
15. Do you have anorexia or bulimia?	☐	☐	☐
16. Do you experience kidney stones?	☐	☐	☐
17. Do you experience leg or knee pain?	☐	☐	☐

The more checkmarks there are in the Always column, the more likely your first chakra is out of balance, under-active, or blocked.

The First Chakra

BASIC SURVIVAL

The first chakra deals with survival instinct, your foundation, grounding and safety issues. It is located at the base of the spine and spins downward toward the ground. It corresponds to the color red, the earth element and the large intestine. Listed below are the qualities of the first chakra depending on whether it is more balanced or unbalanced. Check off those that describe you.

Balanced

∾ Grounded

∾ Dependable

∾ Realistic

∾ Secure

∾ Stable

∾ Balanced

∾ Feeling safe

∾ Practical

Unbalanced

∾ Clingy

∾ Overly stubborn

∾ Spacey

∾ Anorexic (under-active) or Obese (over-active)

∾ Hemorrhoids

∾ Constipation (under-active) or Diarrhea (over-active)

∾ Fearful

∾ Frequently ill or sick

Methods for Opening Your First Chakra

- Wearing red

- Listening to the musical note C

- Walking or hiking outside, especially in nature

- Practicing Yoga (especially leg exercises)

- Dancing or listening to a tribal drum beat

- Imagining your feet are like the roots of a tree

- Eating protein

- Massaging your legs and feet

- Gardening

- Using Feng Shui in your home or office

- Releasing the past

- Letting go of fears

- Element: earth

- Essential Oils: clove, cedarwood, black pepper, vetiver

- Affirmations:

  - I am grounded.

  - I am calm.

  - I have trust.

  - I am safe.

ꝏ Exercise: *The Ballerina* – Stand relaxed, feet wide apart pointing out twelve inches past your shoulders, knees bent. Place your hands on your thighs. Inhale deeply, then as you exhale slowly squat your tailbone toward the floor, keeping your back straight and head up. Allow your hands to slide toward your knees. Do not bring your tailbone past your knees. Hold only for a few seconds, then inhale and straighten your legs up. Repeat ten times.

∾ Exercise: *The Jockey* – Stand with knees slightly bent, feet shoulder width apart, toes facing front, breathing through your mouth. Drop your head forward, chin to chest, then let the rest of your spine slowly follow. Bend forward until your fingers are as close to the floor as possible, keeping your knees bent slightly. Now, while inhaling, lower your hips slowly until your thighs are parallel to the floor. Hold for a few seconds then exhale and straighten your legs, but always keep your knees slightly bent. Continue alternating between the two positions, breathing in when bending down and breathing out when straightening up. Your legs may start to shake or burn. End with your legs straight, but knees still slightly bent. Then begin to straighten slowly, one vertebrae at a time, your head coming up last.

Try this Exercise

The Second Chakra (Your Sacral Chakra)

SELF-ASSESSMENT

Answer the following questions by placing a checkmark under the corresponding column.

	Never	Sometimes	Always
1. Do you experience low back pain?	☐	☐	☐
2. Do you have difficulty with your sexuality?	☐	☐	☐
3. Do you have endometriosis?	☐	☐	☐
4. Do you have a fear of being out of control?	☐	☐	☐
5. Are you overly emotional?	☐	☐	☐
6. Do you experience pre-menstrual syndrome?	☐	☐	☐
7. Are you unemotional?	☐	☐	☐
8. Do you experience erectile dysfunction?	☐	☐	☐
9. Do you experience kidney stones?	☐	☐	☐
10. Do you experience ovarian cysts?	☐	☐	☐
11. Do you experience bladder problems?	☐	☐	☐
12. Do you feel detached from your body?	☐	☐	☐
13. Do you feel like you do not have enough money?	☐	☐	☐
14. Do you feel your life is lacking in abundance?	☐	☐	☐
15. Are you over-controlling?	☐	☐	☐
16. Are you addicted to sex?	☐	☐	☐
17. Are you an alcoholic?	☐	☐	☐
18. Are you addicted to drugs?	☐	☐	☐

The more checkmarks there are in the Always column, the more your second chakra is out of balance, under-active, or blocked.

The Second Chakra

EMOTIONS AND SEXUALITY

The second chakra deals with sexuality and emotions as they relate to relationships concerning intimacy and sensuality. It also governs your pleasure and reproductive system. It is located at the low back and below the navel and corresponds to your genitals, kidneys and bladder. Its color is orange and its element is water. Listed below are the qualities of the second chakra depending on whether it is more balanced or unbalanced. Check off those that describe you.

Balanced

- Expressiveness

- Individuality

- Pleasure

- Relaxation

- Passion

- Charm

Unbalanced

- Sexual organ disorders

- Isolation

- Emotional instability

- Numbness, detached from body

- Over eating (over-active)

- Obsession with sex (over-active)

- Attachment, codependency

- Addictions to food, alcohol or drugs (over-active)

- Bladder or kidney disorders

Methods for Opening Your Second Chakra

- ∾ Wearing orange

- ∾ Listening to the musical note D

- ∾ Being near running water sounds, even indoor waterfalls

- ∾ Drinking six to eight glasses of water per day

- ∾ Dancing, especially belly dancing or Latin dancing

- ∾ Walking

- ∾ Swimming

- ∾ Pampering your body

- ∾ Taking energizing vacations

- ∾ Element: water

- ∾ Essential Oils: sandalwood, ylang ylang, rose

- ∾ Affirmations:
    - ☾ I love my life.
    - ☾ I love my body.
    - ☾ I trust feelings.
    - ☾ I accept myself as I am.

- ∾ Exercise: *Runner's Stretch* – Lunge one leg forward with back leg straight. Bring your pelvis as close to the floor as possible, hands to the outsides of your legs. Remember to keep your front knee parallel with your ankle and not over your front ankle. Lift your head up, look forward and breathe. Hold for twenty seconds. Modified version: back knee will touch the floor.

Try this Exercise

❧ Yoga Posture: *Downward Facing Dog* – Stand with your feet shoulder width apart, knees slightly bent. Slowly bend your body forward at the waist until your hands reach the floor. Walk your hands forward on the floor away from your feet until you are in an upside-down "V" shape. Lift your tailbone to the sky, and press through with your chest so your arms and head are in a straight line. Press your heel into the floor. Breathe and hold. Release by bending your knees to the floor.

Try this Exercise

❧ Exercise: *Upside-down Frog* – Lie on your back, arms out to your sides, bend your knees to your chest, then lower each knee to the floor on each side so the soles of your feet are together. Slowly lower your knees out to your sides. Breathe and feel the weight of your legs pulling them to the floor. Then bring your hand to the inside of your thighs and apply gentle pressure until you feel a stretch. Hold for at least ten seconds and release slowly. End by bringing your knees into your chest.

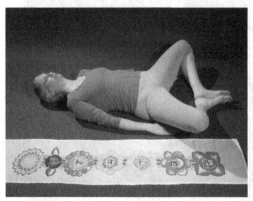

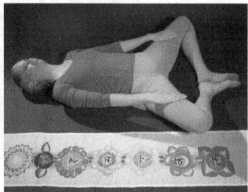

The Third Chakra (Your Solar Plexus Chakra)

SELF-ASSESSMENT

Answer the following questions by placing a checkmark under the corresponding column.

	Never	Sometimes	Always
1. Are you fearful?	☐	☐	☐
2. Are you domineering?	☐	☐	☐
3. Do you experience low self-esteem?	☐	☐	☐
4. Do you have decreased personal power?	☐	☐	☐
5. Do you have decreased will power?	☐	☐	☐
6. Do you lack spontaneity?	☐	☐	☐
7. Are you indecisive?	☐	☐	☐
8. Are you timid?	☐	☐	☐
9. Do you have hepatitis?	☐	☐	☐
10. Do you fear authority figures?	☐	☐	☐
11. Do you fear losing control?	☐	☐	☐
12. Are you experiencing liver disorders?	☐	☐	☐
13. Do you have diabetes?	☐	☐	☐
14. Do you lack joy?	☐	☐	☐
15. Are you afraid to try new things?	☐	☐	☐
16. Do you experience stomach problems?	☐	☐	☐
17. Do you experience gallstones	☐	☐	☐

The more checkmarks there are in the Always column, the more your third chakra is out of balance, under-active, or blocked.

The Third Chakra

PERSONAL POWER AND SELF-ESTEEM

The third chakra relates to your personal power, ego, a strong will and purpose, and your self-esteem. It is located in the center of your body, above your navel. Some cultures call this your Hara, where all energy enters the body. It relates to your stomach, liver, pancreas, and gallbladder. The element is fire and color is yellow. Listed below are the qualities of the third chakra depending on whether it is more balanced or unbalanced. Check off those that describe you.

Balanced

- Enjoying vitality

- Feeling strength of will

- Focused

- Purposeful

- Successful

- Reasonable

- Honest

- Ethical

- Possessing integrity

- High self-esteem

Unbalanced

- Stomach ulcers (under-active) or increased stomach acid (over-active)

- Diabetes

- Hepatitis or Cirrhosis of the liver

- Digestive disorders

- Over-consumption of white sugar or alcohol (over-active)

- Exploiting others/domination/aggression (over-active)

- Being easily exploited/timid (under-active)

Methods for Opening Your Third Chakra

- ✺ Wearing yellow

- ✺ Listening to the musical note E

- ✺ Burning candles

- ✺ Cycling

- ✺ Playing sports, which increases self-esteem

- ✺ Eating hot, spicy foods which increases third chakra energy

- ✺ Imagining a ball of sunshine in front of your Hara center

- ✺ Element: fire

- ✺ Essential Oils: lemon, lemongrass, rosemary, bergamot, lavender

- ✺ Affirmations:
  - ☾ I am worthy.
  - ☾ I am happy.
  - ☾ I am cheerful.
  - ☾ I choose life.

- ✺ Bioenergetic Exercise: *The Woodchopper* – This can be a powerful release for pent up anger. Remove glasses and long necklaces before you begin. Stand with your feet more than shoulder width apart, knees slightly bent. Clasp your hands together and bring them over your head, bending backward slightly. Breathe in as your hands go up and back. Then swiftly on exhale, bring your hands down and through your legs as you loudly voice "Ahh". Come up slowly and repeat seven times. Feel the vibration pulse through your body. Your energy is flowing.

Try this Exercise

The Fourth Chakra (Your Heart Chakra)

SELF-ASSESSMENT

Answer the following questions by placing a checkmark under the corresponding column.

	Never	Sometimes	Always
1. Do you have people in your life to forgive?			
2. Is love lacking in your life?			
3. Is compassion lacking in your life?			
4. Do you feel lonely?			
5. Are you codependent?			
6. Does your heart and mind feel disconnected?			
7. Is there disharmony in your relationships?			
8. Are you emotionally cold and distant?			
9. Have you had breast or lung cancer?			
10. Do you experience heart palpitations?			
11. Do you experience shortness of breath?			
12. Do you have asthma?			
13. Have you had open heart surgery?			
14. Have you been broken hearted?			
15. Do you experience angina?			
16. Do you have heart disease?			
17. Have you experienced a heart attack?			

The more checkmarks there are in the Always column, the more your fourth chakra is out of balance, under-active, or blocked.

The Fourth Chakra

LOVE AND COMPASSIONATE RELATIONSHIPS

The fourth chakra relates to all relationships with love, compassion, intimacy, forgiveness and healing the emotional heart. It governs the heart and lungs and is located in the center of the chest. The element is air and the color is emerald green. Listed below are the qualities of the fourth chakra depending on whether it is more balanced or unbalanced. Check off those that describe you.

Balanced

ᴥ Compassion

ᴥ Acceptance

ᴥ Love

ᴥ Nurturing

ᴥ Understanding

ᴥ Respect

ᴥ Forgiveness

ᴥ Hope

ᴥ Self-care

ᴥ Maintain stable relationships

Unbalanced

ᴥ Loneliness

ᴥ Codependence

ᴥ Overextension of self (over-active)

ᴥ Inability to say No (over-active)

ᴥ Resentment

ᴥ Bitterness

ᴥ Grief

ᴥ Asthma

ᴥ Heart or lung disorders

Methods for Opening Your Fourth Chakra

- ❧ Wearing pink or emerald green

- ❧ Listening to the musical note F

- ❧ Breathing fresh air

- ❧ Focusing on deep breathing – Take five deep breaths every day, inhale through your nose for a count of four, hold for a count of four, and exhale slowly through your mouth with pursed lips, for a count of eight.

- ❧ Releasing unresolved grief – Write a letter to someone you loved who is not in your life anymore.

- ❧ Practicing forgiveness – Practice this journal writing exercise: With a blank piece of paper, start writing "I forgive. I forgive." repeating this phrase until you begin writing something else after it. Let your words flow and do not judge what you write. The goal is to the let the emotion out of your body.

- ❧ Experiencing safe touch

- ❧ Receiving a massage or healing touch session

- ❧ Visualizing a pink heart

- ❧ Tapping or massaging your sternum using your fingertips.

- ❧ Loving yourself

- ❧ Placing items in pairs in your home

- ❧ Practicing kindness

- ❧ Being whatever brings you joy

- ❧ Element: air

- ❧ Essential Oils: rose, lavender, majoram, bergamot, ylang ylang

- ❧ Affirmations:
    - ☾ I am loved.
    - ☾ I have trust.
    - ☾ I have faith.

Any exercise that brings your arms and shoulders back and opens the chest area is helpful to open this chakra.

🐛 Exercise: *Tarzan Roll* – Roll your shoulders forwards five times, then backward five times. Now gently tap your fingers on your sternum. This stimulates your thymus and immune system. If you feel you need to release more, then pound your chest with your fists and yell, "Ahh" like Tarzan did.

🐛 Yoga posture: *Upright Fish* – Sit on the floor with your back straight. Bring your arms behind you and clasp your hands, interlocking your fingers. Bring your shoulders back as you squeeze your shoulder blades together. Lift your chin up and look to the sky, opening your chest. Your hands may rest on the floor. Hold, breathe, then release slowly.

∿ Yoga posture: *Cobra* – Lie face down on the floor, arms bent, hands beside your shoulders, palms down. With your feet together, press your hips into the floor and begin to lift your chest using your arms as little as possible. When you feel your lower body tighten, push your palms into the floor, lift your chest up and point the crown of your head to the sky. Hold, breathe and release slowly.

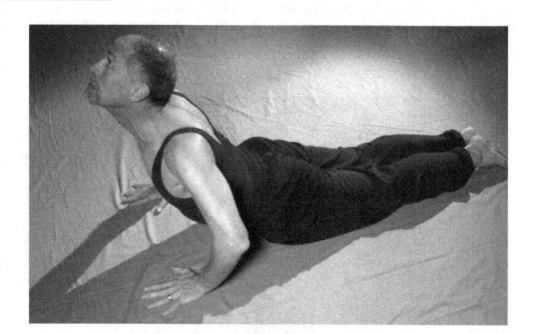

☙ Exercise: *The Archer* – Stand with your feet shoulder width apart, and bring your arms forward in front of you with straight elbows and soft fists touching. One arm at a time, bend each elbow backward behind your body, then forward again to the starting position. Feel the chest area opening. If you feel like there is a monkey on your back, when you bend your elbow backwards loudly say, "Get off my back!". Repeat three times with each arm.

Healing Your Energy

The Fifth Chakra (Your Throat Chakra)

SELF-ASSESSMENT

Answer the following questions by placing a checkmark under the corresponding column.

	Never	Sometimes	Always
1. Do people ask you to speak up louder?	☐	☐	☐
2. Do you feel you have poor communication skills?	☐	☐	☐
3. Do you experience stiff necks?	☐	☐	☐
4. Do you experience sore throats?	☐	☐	☐
5. Are you lacking in creativity?	☐	☐	☐
6. Do you have trouble expressing yourself?	☐	☐	☐
7. Do you have difficulty speaking up for yourself?	☐	☐	☐
8. Do you have difficulty speaking your truth?	☐	☐	☐
9. Do you have difficulty asking for your needs to be met?	☐	☐	☐
10. Do you have a fear of public speaking?	☐	☐	☐
11. Do you have a thyroid disorder?	☐	☐	☐
12. Do you sleep with the TV or music playing?	☐	☐	☐
13. Do you feel like you are not being heard?	☐	☐	☐
14. Do you experience mouth canker sores?	☐	☐	☐

The more checkmarks there are in the Always column, the more your fifth chakra is out of balance, under-active, or blocked.

The Fifth Chakra

EXPRESSION, COMMUNICATION, CREATIVITY

The fifth chakra relates to all types of communication, creativity and vocal expression. It corresponds to the neck, mouth, jaw and throat, sound, music, words and the color bright blue. Listed below are the qualities of the fifth chakra depending on whether it is more balanced or unbalanced. Check off those that describe you.

Balanced

∾ Clear communication

∾ Speaking eloquently

∾ Creativity

∾ Speaking the truth

∾ Expressiveness

∾ Imagination

∾ Higher will/ life purpose

∾ Following your dreams

Unbalanced

∾ Stifled creativity

∾ Difficulty being direct

∾ Poor communication

∾ Speaking instead of listening (over-active)

∾ Telling personal information to strangers (over-active)

∾ Saying every thought that comes into your head (over-active)

∾ Experiencing recurrent sore throats

∾ Feeling neck stiffness

∾ Thyroid disorders

Methods for Opening Your Fifth Chakra

- Wearing bright or turquoise blue

- Listening to the musical note G

- Chanting, toning or making sound

- Singing or laughing

- Playing music

- Journal writing

- Creative painting

- Public speaking

- Teaching

- Praying

- Silent retreats

- Being creative in your life

- Cranio-sacral therapy

- Element: sound

- Essential Oils: eucalyptus, frankincense, sage, chamomile

- Affirmations:
  - ☾ I have joy.
  - ☾ I speak my truth.
  - ☾ I express myself clearly.
  - ☾ I communicate easily.

Try this Exercise

- Exercise: *Chakra Sounds* – Make these sounds sequentially or singularly seven times each. They correspond to each numbered chakra.
  1 o as in soap
  2 oo as in new
  3 ah as in father
  4 ay as in day
  5 ee as in bee
  6 ommm
  7 ngngng as in ding

- Exercise: *Santa Laugh* – Practice fake laughter (ho-ho-ho). Make it loud. Laugh at the top of your lungs. Be free to let the sounds out fully. Laughter increases laughter.

The Sixth Chakra (Your Third Eye Chakra)
SELF-ASSESSMENT

Answer the following questions by placing a checkmark under the corresponding column.

	Never	Sometimes	Always
1. Do you disregard your intuition?	☐	☐	☐
2. Do you experience chronic headaches?	☐	☐	☐
3. Are you lacking in psychic ability?	☐	☐	☐
4. Do you wait for others to tell you what to do?	☐	☐	☐
5. Are you rigid in your thinking?	☐	☐	☐
6. Do you get confused easily?	☐	☐	☐
7. Do you fear seeing spirits or angels?	☐	☐	☐
8. Is your brain constantly thinking?	☐	☐	☐
9. Do you experience pituitary disorders?	☐	☐	☐
10. Are you a negative thinker?	☐	☐	☐
11. Do you speak negatively?	☐	☐	☐
12. Do you lack mental clarity?	☐	☐	☐
13. Are you unable to think for yourself?	☐	☐	☐
14. Do you lack imagination?	☐	☐	☐
15. Do you have poor vision?	☐	☐	☐
16. Do you experience migraines?	☐	☐	☐

The more checkmarks there are in the Always column, the more your sixth chakra is out of balance, under-active, or blocked.

The Sixth Chakra

INTUITION AND IMAGINATION

The sixth chakra relates to illumination, trusting your intuition, your imagination and knowing the unknown. It is located at the brow, or center of your forehead. Also known as your third eye, this is where you may perceive the past or future. It corresponds to the element light and the color indigo blue. Listed below are the qualities of the sixth chakra depending on whether it is more balanced or unbalanced. Check off those that describe you.

Balanced

- Meditative mind

- Knowing the unknown

- Seeing the unseen

- Understanding your destiny

- Psychic perception

- Imagination

- Transcendence

- Spiritual purpose

- Wisdom

- Insight

Unbalanced

- Headaches

- Migraines

- Nightmares

- Hallucinations

- Blindness

- Vision disorders

Methods for Opening Your Sixth Chakra

- ❧ Wearing indigo blue

- ❧ Listening to the musical note A

- ❧ Meditating

- ❧ T'ai Chi Ch'uan

- ❧ Qi gong

- ❧ Journaling your dreams

- ❧ Trusting your intuition

- ❧ Positive thinking, which is proven to help you live longer

- ❧ Imagining your perfect balanced life

- ❧ Visualizing your life in five years – Take the time now to write down a few sentences for your future.

- ❧ Chanting "Om". Practice in a group or by yourself.

- ❧ Element: light

- ❧ Essential Oils: jasmine, peppermint, juniper, rosemary

- ❧ Affirmations:
    - ☾ I trust my intuition.
    - ☾ I am open to wisdom and guidance.
    - ☾ I am wise.
    - ☾ I am compassionate.

Try this Exercise

- ❧ Exercise: *Developing Intuition* – Practice touching, hearing, and seeing with your eyes closed. Practice trusting your intuition. Practice trusting another by being lead around while you are blindfolded.

- ❧ Exercise: *Opening Third Eye* – Sitting comfortably, close your eyes. Place your middle finger at the bridge of your nose between your eyebrows. Slowly push up your finger a couple of inches onto your forehead. Breathing deeply, imagine your third eye opening. Repeat.

The Seventh Chakra (Your Crown Chakra)

SELF-ASSESSMENT

Answer the following questions by placing a checkmark under the corresponding column.

	Never	Sometimes	Always
1. Do you have a lack of understanding?	☐	☐	☐
2. Do you have a lack of knowledge?	☐	☐	☐
3. Do you make unwise choices?	☐	☐	☐
4. Do you feel disconnected to a higher spiritual being?	☐	☐	☐
5. Are you angry at your Creator?	☐	☐	☐
6. Do you feel separate from the world?	☐	☐	☐
7. Are you prejudiced?	☐	☐	☐
8. Do you have a brain disorder?	☐	☐	☐
9. Are you ignoring your body?	☐	☐	☐
10. Have you had negative experiences with organized religion?	☐	☐	☐
11. Are you taking psychiatric medications?	☐	☐	☐
12. Do you feel disconnected with reality?	☐	☐	☐
13. Do you have flighty or spacey behavior?	☐	☐	☐
14. Do you have trouble sleeping?	☐	☐	☐
15. Are you depressed?	☐	☐	☐

The more checkmarks there are in the Always column, the more your seventh chakra is out of balance, under-active, or blocked.

The Seventh Chakra

SPIRITUALITY AND WISDOM

The seventh chakra, also known as the crown chakra, is located on the top of the head and points up to the sky. It relates to understanding, wisdom, knowledge, a higher power and spiritual connection. This chakra corresponds to thought, consciousness, and enlightenment. It responds to the color violet in the west and white in the east. Listed below are the qualities of the seventh chakra depending on whether it is more balanced or unbalanced. Check off those that describe you.

Balanced

- Oneness

- Wisdom

- Understanding

- Knowledge

- Spiritual connection

- Feeling connected

- Divine purpose

- Destiny

- Selflessness

Unbalanced

- Confusion

- Apathy

- Excessive intellectualism (over-active)

- Depression

- Neurological disorders

Methods for Opening Your Seventh Chakra

- ∾ Wearing violet

- ∾ Listening to the musical note B

- ∾ Practicing Yoga

- ∾ T'ai Chi Ch'uan

- ∾ Sufi dancing

- ∾ Prayer

- ∾ Any meditation technique

- ∾ Stillness

- ∾ Reflection

- ∾ Deep breathing

- ∾ Performing rituals

- ∾ Creating an altar

- ∾ Practicing any spiritual belief

- ∾ Element: thought

- ∾ Essential Oils: frankincense, lavender, rose, rosemary, rosewood, sandalwood

- ∾ Affirmations:
    - ☾ I trust my higher power.
    - ☾ I heal for my highest good.
    - ☾ I am limitless.
    - ☾ I have peace.

Try this Exercise

- ∾ Exercise: *The Crown* – Move your right hand with your palm down in a clockwise circular direction two inches above the top of your head. Feel the spiral energy open.

- ∾ Relaxation techniques: *Tense and Relax exercise* – Lie in a comfortable position and close your eyes. Allow your jaw to drop. Take three deep breaths, breathing in through your nose and out through your mouth. Then, starting with your feet, tighten the muscles of your feet and hold for a count of five, then release completely. Continue tightening, holding and releasing the muscles of your body in this order: lower legs, upper legs, buttocks, abdomen, lower back, upper back, hands, arms, shoulders, neck, ending with your face. After tightening and relaxing your entire body, note any areas that still feel tight. Go back to those areas and repeat the exercise. At the end of this exercise, continue with three more deep breaths allowing your body to sink into the surface which supports it. Continue resting for a few more minutes, then slowly open your eyes. This is a wonderful exercise to practice before sleeping.

Methods for Balancing All Your Chakras

- Practicing Yoga postures or T'ai Chi Ch'uan

- Performing the Sun Salutation daily

- Eating whole grain brown rice, chewing thoroughly

- Smudging with white sage to clear negative energy

- Receiving healing hands-on chakra energy balancing

- Receiving Energy Medicine: Reiki, Polarity, Healing Touch, Therapeutic Touch

- Listening to *"Chakra Suite"* by Steven Halpern or *"Rhythms of the Chakras"* by Glen Velez (Sounds True 1998)

- Essential Oils: frankincense, sandalwood

- Affirmation:
  - ☾ My chakras are aligned, opened and perfectly balanced.

Try this Exercise

- Exercise: *Chakra Spinning* – Practice with a partner who is lying on her back. Place your right hand two to four inches above the body, with a flat palm toward the body. Move your hand in a clockwise position over the first chakra; clockwise as you are looking at the person. Feel the pull of the chakra – is it fast or slow? The lower chakras spin slower than the upper chakras. The larger the circle your hand is drawing, the more the energy is flowing through that chakra on that particular day. Begin with the first chakra and work your way up the body to the seventh chakra. You can spin chakras from the front or back of the body. You can also spin your own chakras. Spin your chakras daily for optimal health.

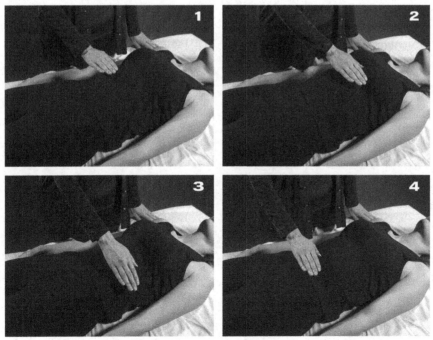

✺ Exercise: *Chakra Balancing* – Practice with a partner who is lying on her back. Place one of your hands on a chakra which feels over-active and the other hand on a different chakra which feels under-active. Your hands can be two inches above the body. Notice the sensations and pull from each chakra. Hold for about three minutes until you feel a change in the energy. Common holds are the second and fourth chakra or the fourth and sixth chakra.

✺ Exercise: *Chakra Clearing* – To pull out old energetic toxins from the chakra, place your hand two inches above a chakra and spin the chakra counterclockwise. You may use a flat palm toward the body or fingertips toward the body to scoop out the toxins. Begin with the first chakra and work your way up the body to the seventh chakra. You may use your right or left hand for clearing. The right hand receives energy and the left hand sends energy. Spin counterclockwise for up to three minutes. Then, always end by spinning the chakra clockwise with your right hand to balance it.

✺ Chakra Meditation Exercise: *Visualization* – Sitting or lying in a comfortable position, close your eyes. Practice visualizing the chakras by color. Imagine them spinning in the direction of the top of your body, to your left, to the bottom of your body, to your right, and back to the top (clockwise). Visualize a cone of each color coming from the chakra area on each exhale.

Begin at your first chakra at the base of your spine and guide your mind up your body toward your seventh chakra at the top of your head. Use the following corresponding colors:

1st - red

2nd - orange

3rd - yellow

4th - green

5th - bright blue

6th - indigo

7th - violet

Chakra Meditation

The meditation below will only take a few minutes and balances your chakras. You may read it into a voice recorder using a slow, calm voice and then play it back whenever you need balance in your life.

Lie comfortably on a bed or carpeted floor.

Notice your breath. Breathe in through your nose, deep into your belly, then exhale slowly and fully through your mouth.

See yourself surrounded in white healing light, covering you like a soft cloud. The white light spins around you, protecting your body.

Bring your attention to your first chakra, your root chakra. It spins from your tailbone down toward your feet, opening like an ice cream cone. See the energy as red and spinning in a clockwise direction, opening, balancing and grounding you. Releasing and renewing.

Bring your attention to your second chakra, below your belly button. It spins out of the front and back of your body in a clockwise direction, opening like an ice cream cone. See the energy as orange and healing your power and controlling relationships, opening and balancing your sexuality. Releasing and renewing.

Bring your attention to your third chakra, your solar plexus, above your belly button. It spins out of the front and back of your body in a clockwise direction, opening like an ice cream cone. See the energy as sun yellow and feeling your self-esteem and will power increasing, opening and balancing your personal power. Releasing and renewing.

Bring your attention to your fourth chakra, your heart and lungs. It spins out the front and back of your body in a clockwise direction, opening like an ice cream cone. See the energy as emerald green and healing your love and compassionate relationships. Feel it opening, balancing, and releasing your past with joy while renewing your passion for love.

Bring your attention to your fifth chakra, at your throat. It spins out of the front and back of your body in a clockwise direction, opening like an ice cream cone. See the energy as bright blue and speaking your truth, opening and balancing your creativity. Releasing and renewing.

Bring your attention to your sixth chakra, in the center of your forehead. It spins out of the front and back of your body in a clockwise direction, opening like an ice cream cone. See the energy as purple, hearing and trusting your intuition and imagination, opening and balancing your third eye of insight. Releasing and renewing.

Bring your attention to your seventh chakra, your crown chakra, spinning out of the top of your head toward the sky opening like an ice cream cone. See the energy as violet and connecting you to the healing energy of the universe. Opening and balancing. Releasing and renewing.

Feel all of your chakras spinning together, perfectly opened and balanced. You are calm and clear. Your energy flows in and around you.

When you are ready, take your time and slowly bring your focus back to the room. Rise slowly and intentionally, noticing how you feel.

Write a description of how your body feels.

SECTION II - REIKI I: FIRST DEGREE

Chapter 4
Reiki First Degree

Introduction to Reiki

After having studied many different types of energy work including Therapeutic Touch and Polarity, I have chosen to present Reiki in this introduction to energy guidebook because it is so easy to learn and use. No memorization of specific body points is needed. Reiki is performed by health care professionals, including nurses and massage therapists, throughout the world. As a massage therapist, knowing a form of energy work diversifies your practice. It allows you to be able to provide hands-on bodywork to clients who would rather be fully dressed, or you can incorporate Reiki into any massage session.

Reiki is one specific type of energy work. It is the only one I know where you receive energy by a process called an attunement. I have studied other methods of energy therapy, and Reiki resonated with me because it is effortless. Place your hands on someone who chooses to heal, and the Reiki healing energy is there. I believe healing is that simple.

Reiki is hands-on healing utilizing the Universal Life Force energy. This is the energy which surrounds all of us. If each one of us used Reiki on ourselves and others every day, maybe we could heal the earth.

I was first intrigued by Reiki because of self healing. Reiki begins with self healing before we heal others. I know it has changed my life 100% for the better. I believe we all have some part of our self which needs to be reconnected.

Reiki energy can help create balance in our dis-eased energy. Today, Reiki is used by many people all over the world. There are thousands of Reiki Masters in the United States. Reiki Level I and II training can be completed in a few days and the attunement lasts a lifetime. Reiki is so safe and gentle even a baby may be attuned and will always have the Reiki healing energy. I believe this is one of the ways we can help heal ourselves and others.

Reiki healing can be subtle, yet profound. Whenever an injured person appears in my life, I place my hands on them and can feel the Reiki energy begin to flow immediately. I can always assist and say, "Reiki be with me". The Reiki energy calms the person and begins the healing process.

Everything which has energy can benefit by receiving Reiki healing energy. I have performed Reiki on adults, children, animals, plants, buildings, computers and car engines. All have benefited by balanced and increased energy.

What is Reiki?

Reiki   (pronounced Ray-Key) is a Japanese word meaning "Universal Life Energy".

Reiki   is natural healing energy that brings the body into balance and harmony.

Reiki   is noninvasive hands-on healing.

Reiki   assists in healing the physical, mental, emotional, and spiritual being.

Reiki   may be practiced in conjunction with any medical diagnosis. It is safe to use
          with medical treatments or medications.

Reiki   always works for the person's highest good and never brings harm to the
          giver or receiver.

Reiki   balances the chakras and relieves blockages.

Reiki   does not interfere with any religious belief and is not a religious practice.

Reiki   is safe for adults, children, animals, and plants.

Rei   means universal

Ki   is the energy or life force which flows through every living thing. It is known as:

     ❨   Chi to the Chinese

     ❨   Prana to Hindus

Benefits of Reiki

BENEFITS MAY INCLUDE:

☾ Reducing stress

☾ Relaxation

☾ Decreasing pain

☾ Improving circulation

☾ Minimizing recovery time from surgery

☾ Optimizing health

☾ Reducing healing time

☾ Healing from emotional trauma

☾ Quickening physical healing

☾ Increasing mental healing

☾ Enhancing energy

☾ Balancing chakras

☾ Reducing medication side effects

☾ Providing clearer direction

☾ Improving clarity and focus

☾ Feeling more grounded

☾ Experiencing safe touch

Reiki Attunements

Reiki energy cannot be taught. It is a transference of energy. Attunements open you up to be a channel for Reiki energy. Think of it as being tuned to a new radio station, "WREI". After the attunement, you can channel Reiki healing energy. To become a Reiki practitioner, one needs to receive attunements from a third degree Reiki Master Teacher. Traditionally, Reiki attunements were always performed face to face with your Master Teacher. Today, attunements may be received over the phone or via the internet. Each student has to decide for herself what kind of attunement and teaching they require. I currently only provide attunements in a classroom setting.

During an attunement, the Reiki Master Teacher puts Reiki symbols into your energy field using meditation, breath, and touch. The attunement lasts a few minutes and provides a sense of calm and lightness. It may be done in a group or one on one with the Master Teacher.

After each attunement, it takes at least three weeks for your being to adjust to this new level. Each chakra clears for about three days for a total of 21 days of clearing. Students may keep a journal for the first 21 days to relate the clearing of each chakra. Notice physical or emotional changes that surface and allow for opportunities to release the energy.

Reiki I - first degree

In Reiki Level I, the student receives four attunements which produce a 20% to 25% power transference. This energy is for physical healing and especially self healing. Reiki I may be practiced for three weeks before receiving Reiki II attunements.

Reiki II - second degree

In Reiki Level II, the student receives another attunement which is a 100% power transference. This level heals the emotional and mental being. Symbols are taught to perform absent healing from a distance. It takes at least six months for your being to adjust to the emotional clearing process. It may take up to four years, depending upon the amount of emotional baggage you are clearing. Many people receive only the level I and II attunements. Some Reiki I and II classes are taught together in a weekend. It is a personal preference of teachers and students if they prefer time to adjust between first and second degree Reiki classes.

Reiki III - third degree

In Reiki Master Teacher Training, an additional attunement is received which brings the person to the master level. The master level is the highest attunement. A master receives more symbols to help heal. The teacher level allows a person to pass attunements. One should practice Reiki II until comfortable and be fully adjusted before becoming a Reiki Master Teacher. Sometimes this is taught as two levels: Reiki III Master and Reiki IV Reiki Teacher.

The History of Reiki

When I was taught Reiki I in 1994, the history of Dr. Mikao Usui was portrayed as a story told through the generations. Since then many people have researched the facts and real life of Dr. Usui. Entire books are now written on the history of Reiki. The following is a brief description of the facts as I currently know them about the history of how Reiki was discovered.

Dr. Mikao Usui, a Japanese Buddhist monk, discovered and developed Reiki. He was born August 15, 1865 in Japan and died March 9, 1926 in Japan.

His business career took a turn for the worse in 1914, and he became a Buddhist monk. He traveled throughout Japan, China, and Europe seeking knowledge from 1914 to 1922. Dr. Usui was looking for the key to healing without draining his own energy.

Dr. Usui decided to climb Mount Kurama in Japan, where he had studied meditation as a boy, to fast and meditate for 21 days. He used 21 stones to count the days. He took one stone away at the end of each day. This was in March 1922.

As the story goes, on the 21st day, as he was meditating, Dr. Usui saw a bright light coming toward him. It seemed to hit him in the head and he was knocked to the ground unconscious. When he came to, he saw millions of rainbow bubbles with Sanskrit symbols in them. He had been attuned and knew he could heal others without depleting his own energy. He called this healing ability Usui Reiki Ryoho.

Dr. Usui meditated every day to balance his energy. He lived by the Reiki Principles.

In April 1922, Dr. Usui moved to Tokyo and started a healing society he named "Usui Reiki Ryoho Gakkai". He also opened a Reiki healing clinic. He taught classes and gave Reiki treatments. In 1925, after Japan's largest earthquake, the need for Reiki healing increased and he opened a larger clinic in Tokyo.

Dr. Usui trained 16 teachers. He died March 9, 1926 of a stroke. There is a Usui Memorial established for him in Japan.

Dr. Chujiro Hayashi was one of the teachers trained by Dr. Usui. He took over the Tokyo clinic when Dr. Usui died.

In 1936, Hawayo Takata came from Hawaii to the clinic to receive Reiki healing. After she was healed, she learned Reiki from Dr. Hayashi and was attuned. In 1937, Hawayo Takata returned to Hawaii and began teaching Reiki and giving treatments. Later she opened two clinics in Hawaii. She is responsible for bringing Reiki to America.

In Japan a nominal fee is charged for Reiki training. In 1970, Hawayo Takata named the Reiki III training "Master" and began charging $10,000 for the education. She initiated 22 Reiki masters before she died in December 1980.

In the 1980's, some of the Masters Trained by Mrs. Takata felt that Reiki should be available to everyone. They initiated giving away Reiki training and attunements and it grew quickly in America.

In 1982, Phyllis Lei Furomoto, Takata's granddaughter, started the Reiki Alliance.

In the 1990's, William Lee Rand founded The International Center for Reiki Training in Michigan. The newsletter *Reiki News* is sent to more that 72,000 people and is available at: www.reiki.org

Today there are thousands of Reiki practitioners and Reiki Masters all over the world.

*Today, I will give thanks
for my many blessings.*

Today, I will not worry.

Today, I will not be angry.

Today, I will do my work honestly.

*Today, I will be kind to my neighbor
and every living thing.*

This is the meditation that Dr. Usui practiced every morning and evening. Say it every morning when you rise and notice how your day unfolds.

Your Reiki Lineage

Fill in your Reiki Lineage. Begin with one of the 22 masters attuned by Hawayo Takata. Then write in the name of the Reiki Master attuned by her until you reach your Reiki Masters name. Then write your name at the bottom.

Dr. Mikao Usui

Dr. Chujiro Hayashi

Hawayo Takata

_____

_____

_____

_____

_____

_____

_____

_____

_____

_____

Reiki Meditation

Practice meditation everyday. Mediation can be done for 15 to 30 minutes a day, once or twice a day. The purpose is to enhance your energy. It is always helpful to meditate before giving a Reiki session. Dr. Usui meditated daily.

- Practice meditation by sitting comfortably. Place your palms on your body or touch your palms together and place them in front of your heart center.

- Inhale through your nose and exhale slowly through your mouth during the meditation. One type of count is to inhale for four, hold for four, and exhale for eight counts. Exhale with pursed lips (like blowing up a balloon).

- Close your eyes, and sit in a relaxed position with your back as straight as possible. It is okay to lean against a wall. Breathe deeply into your belly when you inhale.

If you are participating in a Reiki I class, this is the point in time when you will receive your attunements. Afterwards, discuss or write down how you felt during your attunement.

Reiki Spirit Guides

- A guide is a spirit which helps the practitioner use her intuition for where to place her hands and how long to keep them at a particular location on the body.

- A Reiki spirit guide is assigned to every practitioner when they receive First Degree Reiki.

- Reiki guides assist in all attunements.

- More guides will be assigned with the Second and Third Degree.

- Their purpose is to help practitioners use Reiki for the good of all.

- They send the practitioner messages about the receiver, like where to place your hands.

- The receiver may feel like more hands are on their body than only those of the practitioner.

- The receiver may say they can still feel your hands after you have removed them from the receiver's body.

- Reiki guides are present in all Reiki healing sessions.

- You can ask for the guides help during a healing session.

- Meditation is one method of connecting with your spirit guides.

- Practice being aware of Reiki guides, and you will notice them more.

The Reiki Prayer

This technique teaches you to follow your intuition. Use it before a Reiki session.

- ❧ Sit or stand comfortably and close your eyes

- ❧ Place your hands, in prayer position in front of your heart. Breathe deeply and ask the Reiki energy to flow through you

- ❧ Ask for Reiki healing energy to gently heal your client's physical, emotional and spiritual body.

- ❧ Lift your hands up to your third eye. Breathe deeply and ask for your hands to be guided to where on the body your client needs healing.

- ❧ Lightly place your hands on your clients body. Trust your intuition.

Preparing for a Reiki Session

- ✺ have a quiet, uninterrupted, safe space

- ✺ practice meditation first

- ✺ wash hands with soap and water before giving a full body treatment

- ✺ if wearing a watch, remove it

- ✺ client can be lying down on a table, such as a massage table

- ✺ client can be sitting in a low back chair

- ✺ client is usually fully clothed

- ✺ find a comfortable position, and if sitting, make sure legs are uncrossed

- ✺ keep fingers and thumbs together

- ✺ full body treatment takes 40 to 90 minutes

- ✺ call in Reiki guides to help for the client's highest good

Giving a Reiki Treatment

- ❧ wash your hands

- ❧ gently place both hands on the body; no pressure is needed

- ❧ your hands may become very hot

- ❧ hold each position for three to five minutes, trust your intuition and your hands; they will tell you when it is time to move

- ❧ injured areas may be held for 10 to 20 minutes

- ❧ if organs or limbs are missing, treat as if they were there

- ❧ broken bones should be set in a cast first, then place your hands directly over the cast

- ❧ pets and children may only need a position held for 30 seconds; they will let you know

- ❧ after the treatment, wash your hands for 20 to 30 seconds in cool water to break the energy flow

- ❧ perform energy releasing techniques for yourself

- ❧ a full body Reiki treatment will balance the chakras

Receiving a Reiki Treatment

- ∾ remove jewelry, watch, eyeglasses, belts, and shoes

- ∾ may remain dressed

- ∾ sit or lie down in a comfortable position

- ∾ place a pillow under knees or ankles for comfort

- ∾ make sure feet and legs stay uncrossed

- ∾ after the treatment, drink five ounces of water

Rules of Reiki

- ∾ always ask if the person wants Reiki healing

- ∾ do not give Reiki away; trade for something if not being paid

Chapter 5
Reiki Sequence for Self

Hand Positions for Treating Oneself

At the core of healing others is healing yourself first. Reiki is designed for you to treat yourself. As the Reiki energy opens your chakras and balances your own energy system, it allows self healing to begin. Healing does begin with yourself. Once you are exploring your healing path, then you can be a clearer channel for energy flow and help others to heal themselves.

After being attuned to Reiki Level I, practice Reiki on yourself every night. Before you fall asleep, place your hands on a Reiki position which calls to you. Continue to other positions until you are asleep. You will find your hands automatically flow to the areas of your body that need healing. The more you use Reiki, the stronger the energy and your intuition will become. I still wake up many mornings with my hands on my body in a Reiki position. I know I am receiving what I need.

Front Side (Can be performed sitting or lying on your back.)

1. *Both hands over the eyes.*
   For eyes and sinuses.

2. *Hands on sides of face.*
   Either over the cheeks, in front of the ears or over the temples.
   For stress and headaches.

2a. *Alternative hands on sides of face.*
    Fingertips touching on top of head.
    For crown chakra.

3.   *Hands on back of the head.*
     For eyes, headaches, fear, third eye chakra.

3a.   *Alternative hands on back of head.*

4. *Hands on front of the throat.*
   For throat disorders, thyroid, communication, self-expression, 5th chakra.

5. *Hands over the heart/thymus (breastbone).*
   For heart, thymus, lung, emotions, allergies, asthma, 4th chakra.

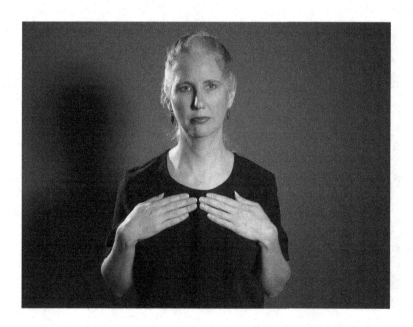

5a.   *Alternative hands over heart.*

6.   *Hands over the lower ribs below breasts.*
     For liver, gallbladder, pancreas, immune system, diabetes.

7. *Hands over abdomen, one on each side, or each side separately with both hands. For intestines, digestion, solar plexus, 3rd chakra.*

8. *Hands over lower abdomen, pelvic bones, in a V-shape. For bladder, ovaries, appendix, 2nd chakra.*

9. *Hands over both knees.*
   For joint problems and support.

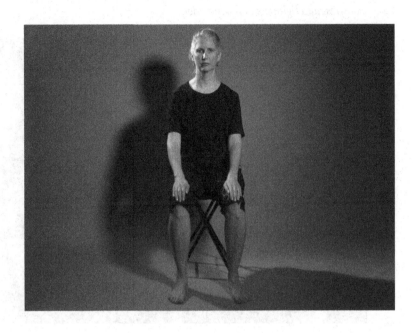

10. *Hands over knee and ankle.*
    For grounding the energy down.

Back Side (Can be performed sitting.)

11. *Hands on back of the neck and over the top of shoulders.*
    For stress and tightness in the shoulders.

12. *Hands on lower ribs.*
    For nerves, lung, backaches.

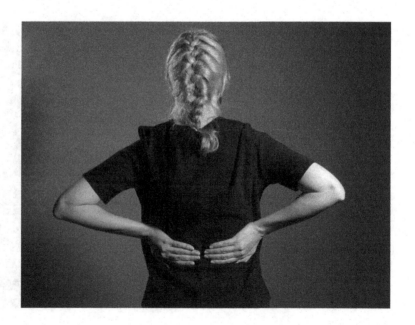

13. *Hands on middle back at waist.*
    For nerves, kidneys, backaches.

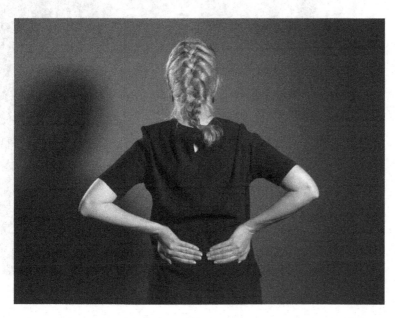

14. *Hands on lower back at hips.*
    For nerves, backaches, hip, sciatica.

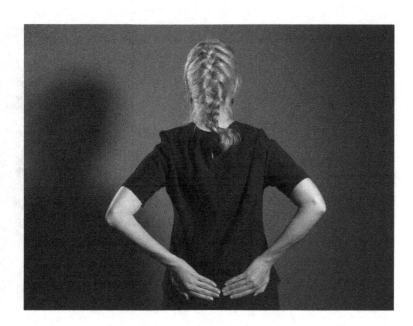

15.　Hands on buttocks at sacrum.
　　　For nerves, backaches, hip, sciatica.

16.　Hands on the soles of both feet.
　　　For grounding the energy down.

16a. *Alternative hands on the soles of one foot at a time.*

Chapter 6
Reiki Sequence for Others

Hand Positions for Treating Others

In Reiki I, the focus of healing others is in the physical body. However the client may experience relief on the mental level also. Practice full body Reiki, but allow your hands to move to specific areas on the body which require additional attention. The same hand positions are utilized in Reiki II.

Front Side/Supine (Receiver lying on her back.)

1. *Both hands over the eyes. For eyes and sinuses.*

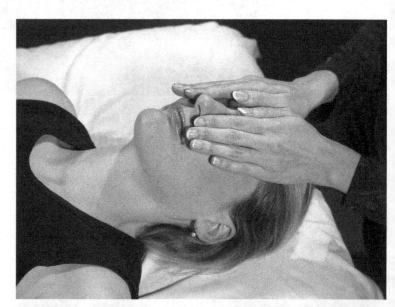

2. *Hands on sides of face. Either over the cheeks, in front of the ears or over the temples. For stress and headaches.*

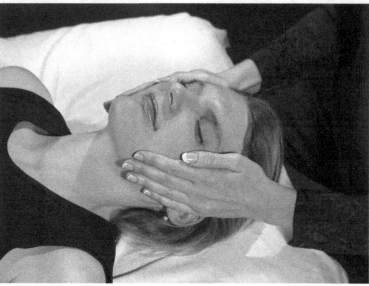

2a. *Alternative hands on sides of face.*
Wrist touching at top of head and fingertips to the temples.
For crown chakra.

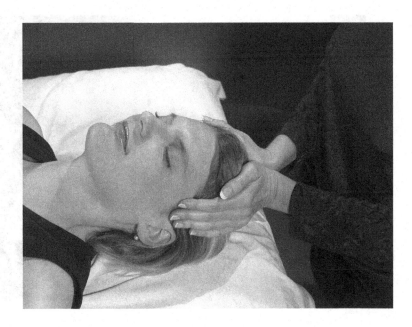

3. *Hands on back of the head.*
Can be performed lying face up or face down.
For eyes, headaches, fear, third eye chakra.

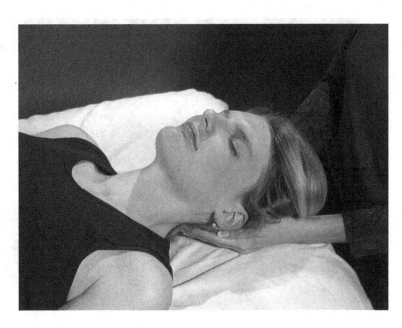

4.   *Hands on front of the throat.*
     For throat disorders, thyroid, communication, self-expression, 5th chakra.

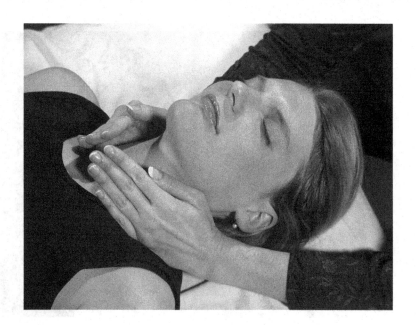

5.   *Hands over the heart/thymus (breastbone).*
     For heart, thymus, lung, emotions, allergies, asthma, 4th chakra.

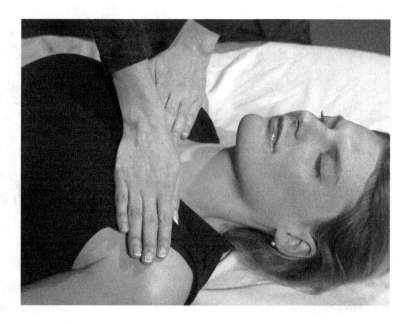

5a. *Alternative hands over heart.*

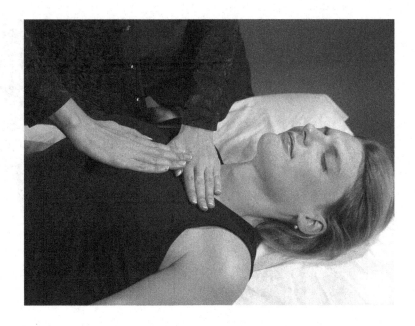

6. *Hands over the lower ribs below breasts.*
For liver, gallbladder, pancreas, immune system, diabetes.

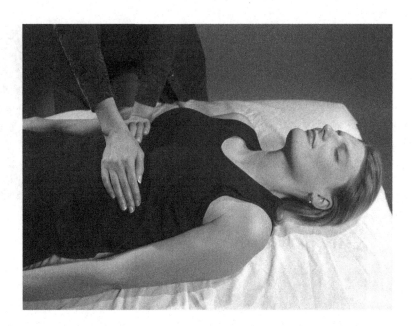

7. *Hands over abdomen, one on each side, or each side separately with both hands. For intestines, digestion, solar plexus, 3rd chakra.*

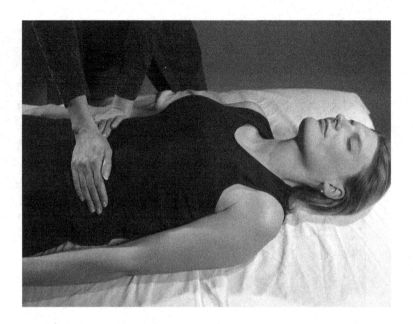

7a. *Alternative hands over abdomen.*

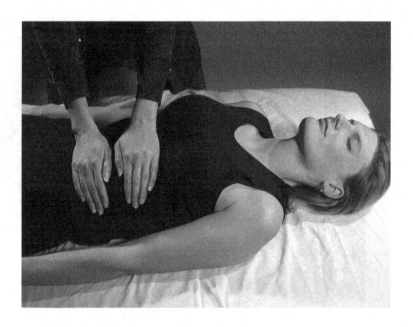

8. *Hands over lower abdomen, pelvic bones, in a V-shape.*
   For bladder, ovaries, appendix, 2nd chakra.

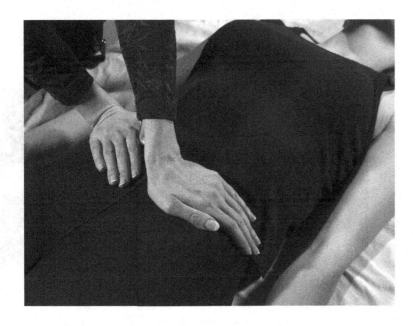

9. *Hands over knees. For joint problems and support.*

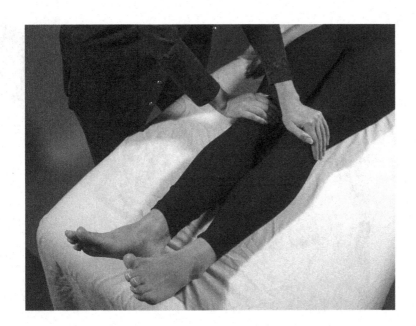

10. *Hands over ankles.*
    For grounding the energy down.

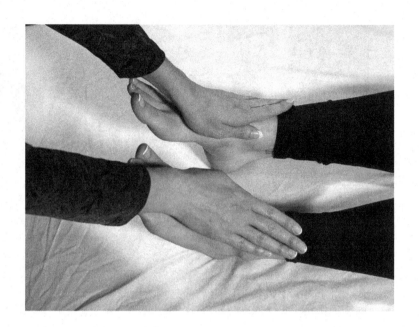

10a. *Alternative hands on knee and foot.*

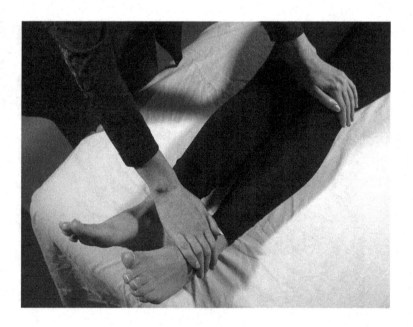

Back Side/Prone (Receiver lying on her abdomen.)

11. *Hands on back of head. For headaches.*

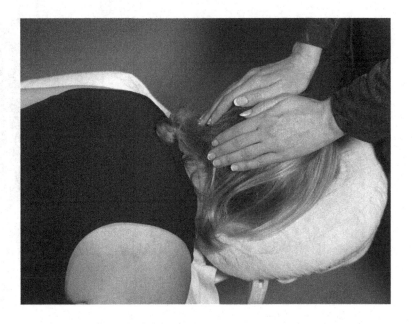

12. *Hands on back of the neck and over the top of shoulders.*
    For stress and tightness in the shoulders.

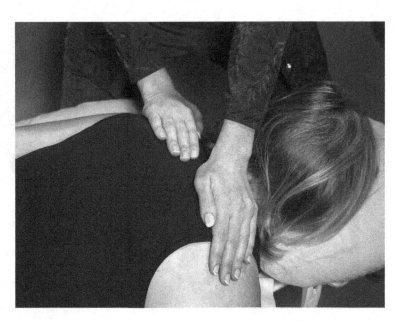

13. *Hands on lower ribs.*
    For nerves, lung, backaches.

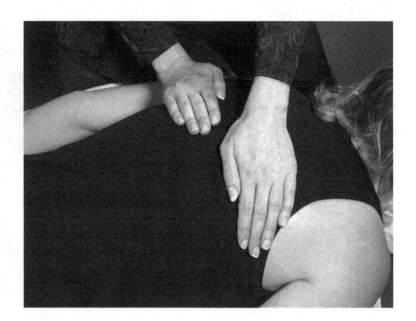

14. *Hands on middle back at waist.*
    For nerves, kidneys, backaches.

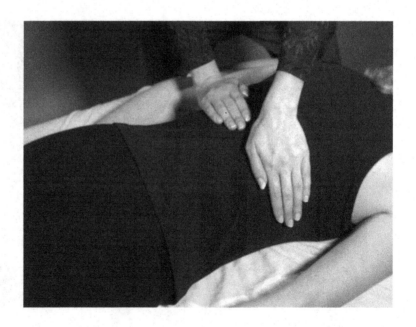

15. *Hands on lower back at hips.*
For nerves, backaches, hip, sciatica.

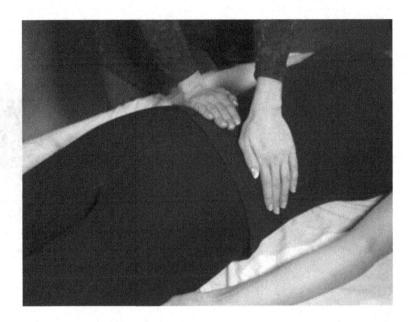

16. *Hands on buttocks at sacrum.*
For nerves, backaches, hip, sciatica.

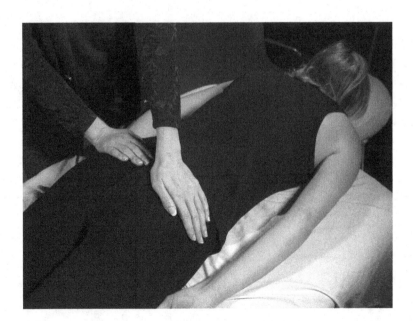

17. *Hands on the soles of both feet.*
    For grounding the energy down.

Chapter 7
Reiki Second Degree

In Second Degree Reiki you will:

- ✺ learn three symbols and how to use them
- ✺ learn distant or absentee healing
- ✺ receive an attunement

About Second Degree Reiki:

- ✺ it is for emotional and mental healing
- ✺ there are Traditional and modern Reiki methods
- ✺ it may take at least six months to integrate the self healing
- ✺ the sacred symbols are from the Sanskrit language
- ✺ the symbols must be treated with respect
- ✺ Reiki symbols cannot be misused
- ✺ no harm can occur when using the symbols
- ✺ Reiki guides will make themselves known
- ✺ the guidance becomes conscious

If you are participating in a Reiki II class, this is the point in time when you will receive your attunements. Discuss or write down how you felt during your attunement.

About the symbols:

∾ they are the keys to using and passing on this healing system

∾ three are taught in Second Degree Reiki and two more are taught in Third Degree Reiki

∾ they can be used in direct hands-on healing, self healing, and distant healing

Reiki symbols have always been considered sacred and secret. When I was attuned in 1994, you could not find a copy of the symbols without taking a Reiki class. Today the symbols are available in print and on the internet. I still believe the symbols are sacred and need to be treated with respect. I have chosen not to print the Reiki symbols in this book. The symbols will be available to you through your Reiki Master Teacher.

How to use the symbols:

∾ they must be memorized and drawn exactly

∾ intent is extremely important

∾ say them as you draw them

∾ visualize them as if in a meditation

∾ draw them in the air with the whole hand, not just a finger

∾ draw them at the beginning of a session or over the receiver's body or draw them on the roof of your mouth with your tongue

∾ to increase the power of the symbols, place your tongue against the roof of your mouth behind the teeth to connect the two Kundalini/Hara energy channels of the body (front and back channels).

When your Reiki Master Teacher shows you the symbols, draw each one on a piece of paper until you can draw it with your eyes closed. Then practice drawing each symbol in the air while saying its name three times.

The Three Symbols

The Power Symbol

- used to increase power

- focuses on healing the physical body

- concentrates Reiki in one focused spot

- Modern symbol
    - drawn clockwise, moving left to right

- Traditional symbol
    - drawn counterclockwise, right to left

- Northern Hemisphere
    - clockwise is used to increase counterclockwise is used to decrease

- Southern Hemisphere
    - clockwise is used to decrease counterclockwise is used to increase

- pick the way that resonates with you and use it consistently

Mental Emotional Healing Symbol

- used for emotional healing

- aligns the upper chakras

- specifically addresses healing the emotional body

- used in most healing sessions

- works with the subconscious

- other uses:
  - protection and purification
  - clearing negative energy
  - releasing spirit attachments
  - guarding a room against negative emotions, disease, or entities

Distant Healing Symbol

- used for absent or distance healing

- representation of the chakras or fire elements in a statue or building form

- means "No past, no present, no future"

- most powerful of the Reiki II symbols

- energy transmits Reiki healing across distance, space, and time

- can be used for hands-on healing for self and others

- works with the conscious mind

- heals the mental body

- can heal the past, present, and future in this and other lifetimes

- using the symbol doubled, two images drawn side by side, accesses and heals the future

Clearing with Reiki Symbols

Use these symbols together for clearing and increasing energy.

Draw the Emotional Symbol first, then the Power Symbol.

- Use over **food** to cleanse if its freshness is in question (Emotional Symbol), and to increase nutritional value (Power Symbol).

- Use over **medicine** to increase healing properties and decrease possible side effects. Hold the medicine in your hand and send it the Emotional Symbol, then the Power Symbol.

- To clear **crystals**, hold the crystal and visualize sending the Emotional Symbol; repeat as needed, and then send the Power Symbol.

- To clear a **house or room**, use the Emotional Symbol over the windows, doors, and at the corners of a house or room to clear the energy. Use the Power Symbol in each room to promote a peaceful home.

- Use this same clearing outside the house, or on a **car**.

Distant Healing with Reiki

- ✑ you must have permission to send distant healing

- ✑ if you have not asked the person to be treated directly, you can ask them energetically

- ✑ meditate and visualize them

- ✑ ask if they want healing

- ✑ you will receive an answer; it could be a voice, or you may see them turning toward or away from you

- ✑ proceed only when you have received permission

- ✑ use this for people and animals

When to Use Distant Healing

- ✑ the person is not physically present

- ✑ the person cannot be touched because of pain; for example: has a burn

- ✑ there is risk of an infection being spread

- ✑ the animal is not a pet and may be dangerous

Sending a Distant Healing

A healing can be sent once or twice a day if needed. There are many methods to send distant or absentee healing.

Here are two different methods:

METHOD ONE

- ∾ visualize someone in need of healing
- ∾ use a photograph or object that reminds you of that person, or write her name on a piece of paper. Hold that object in your hands.
- ∾ come into a meditative state
- ∾ ask permission from the universe
- ∾ send the healing energy to the person, not to their disease
- ∾ visualize and send the symbols in this order:
    - ☾ Distant Healing Symbol
    - ☾ The Power Symbol
    - ☾ The Emotional Healing Symbol
- ∾ ask the Reiki guides if there is anything else you can do for this person
- ∾ always be positive and thankful
- ∾ come out of the meditative state

METHOD TWO

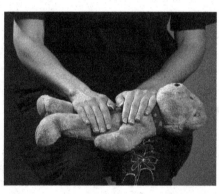

- ∾ use a teddy bear, doll or pillow
- ∾ visualize the person in need of healing
- ∾ ask permission
- ∾ draw the three symbols over the object, always starting with the Distant Healing Symbol
- ∾ imagine doing a hands-on healing by putting your hands on the object
- ∾ the object's body parts correspond to the person's body parts
- ∾ the positions can be held as if you were with the person
- ∾ the healing can take place while you are doing other things, like watching TV
- ∾ hold each position until you feel it is time to change

Clearing Chakras: During a distant healing, you may ask to see the chakras. If a chakra is cloudy or unbalanced, you can clear and balance each chakra by sending the Emotional Healing Symbol.

Chapter 8
Specific Reiki Treatments

It is always recommended that a full Reiki treatment be given. Afterwards, extra time may be spent on the following positions. For any illness not listed, place hands directly over the affected area. Remember, Reiki is used in combination with medical treatment and does not replace contacting a physician for any chronic illness. Reiki is safe to use in combination with any treatment or medication regime.

Photos for the hand positions are found at the end of this chapter.

Abscess	- Front #1, place hands over area
Acne	- Head #1,3 Front #4 Back #3
Addictions	- Head #1,2,3 Front #2
Addison's Disease	- Front #1,2 Back #3
Adhesions	- place hands over area
Aging	- Head #3 Front #1 Back #3
AIDS	- Head #2,3 Front #1,2,3 Back #2,3
Allergies	- Head #1 Front #2 Back #3
ALS	- Head #2,3
Alzheimer's	- Head #1,2,3 Front #2
Amnesia	- Head #2
Anemia	- Head #1 Front #1,3
Anger	- Front #1 Back #3
Angina	- Front #1,2 Back #2
Anorexia Nervosa	- Head #2,3
Anxiety	- Head #1 Front #2 Back #3
Aphasia	- Head #2
Appendicitis	- Front #3 Back #3
Arteriosclerosis	- Head #4 Front #1,4
Arthritis	- Head #2,3 Back #3
Asthma	- Head #3 Back #1
Autism	- Head #1,3
Backache	- Back #4
Baldness	- Head #2 Front #4
Bell's Palsy	- Head #2
Bereavement	- Head #2,3 Front #2
Blood pressure	- Head #3 Back #1,3
Bronchitis	- Front #1 place hands on either side of chest
Bulimia	- Head #2,3
Cancer	- Head #3 Front #1,2 place hands over specific areas
Candida Albicans	- Head #3 Front #1,4
Carpal Tunnel Syndrome	- place hands above and below wrist
Cataracts	- Head #1,3
Cerebral Palsy	- Head #1,2,3
Chemotherapy	- Head #1,2 Front #1 Back #3
Childbirth	- Front #3,4
Chicken Pox	- Front #1 Back #3

Cholesterol	- Head #2 Back #3 Front #2
Circulation	- Front #1 Back #2
Cirrhosis	- Front #2,3 Back #2
Claustrophobia	- Head #1,2,3
Colds	- Head #1,2,4 Front #1
Colon Disorders	- Front #2,3,4
Compulsive Behavior	- Head #3 Front #1,2
Congestive Heart Failure	- Front #1,2 Back #3
Conjunctivitis	- Head #1 Front #1 Back #2
Constipation	- Front #3,4 Back #4
Convulsions	- Head #2 Front #2
Crohn's Disease	- Front #3,4
Cushing's Disease	- Head #2 Back #3
Cystitis	- Front #4
Dandruff	- Head #2,3
Deafness	- Head #2,3
Depression	- Head #2
Dementia	- Head #1
Dermatitis	- Front #1 place hands over affected area
Diabetes	- Front #3 Back #2,3
Diarrhea	- Front #3,4
Digestion	- Head #2,3 Front #2 Back #3
Down's Syndrome	- Head #1,2,3
Duodenal Ulcer	- Front #2 Back #3 Head #3
Dyslexia	- Head #2,3
Dysmenorrhea	- Front #4 Back #4
Earache	- Head #2,4
Eczema	- Head #1 Back #3
Edema	- Front #1,2 Back #3
Emphysema	- Front #1,2 Back #2
Endometriosis	- Front #4 Back #4
Epilepsy	- Head #2 Front #2
Fever	- Front #1,2 Back #3
Fear	- Head #3 Front #2 Back #3
Flu	- Head #3,4 Front #1
Food Poisoning	- Front #2,3,4
Gallbladder	- Front #2,3
Gallstones	- Front #2,3
Gingivitis	- Head #1 sides of jaw
Glaucoma	- Front #1
Gout	- Back #3
Hallucinations	- Head #1,2,3
Hangover	- Head #1,2,3 Front #1,3 Back #3
Headaches	- Head #1,2,3
Heart Murmur	- Front #1 Back #2
Heartburn	- Front #2
Heatstroke	- Head #2,3
Hemophilia	- Front #2 Back #2
Hepatitis	- Front #1,2,3
Herpes	- Front #1 Back #3
Hyperactivity	- Head #2,3

Hyperthyroidism	- Front #4
Hypochondria	- Head #3 Back #3
Hypothermia	- Head #2 Front #2 Back #3
Hypothyroidism	- Head #4
Immunodeficiency	- Front #1,2 Back #2
Incontinence	- Front #4
Impotence	- Head #3 Back #4 Front #4
Indigestion	- Front #2,3 Back #3
Infection	- Front #1
Infertility	- Front #4 Back #4
Insomnia	- Head #3
Irritable Bowel Syndrome	- Head #3 Back #4 Front #4
Jaundice	- Front #2,3
Kidney Problems	- Back #3
Laryngitis	- Head #4
Leukemia	- Head #2,3 Front #1,2 Back #2,3
Lung Problem	- Front #1,2 Back #2
Lupus Erythematosis	- Head #2 Front #1 Back #3
Lymphoma	- Front #1,2 Back #3
Macular Degeneration	- Head #1,3
Manic Depression	- Head #1,2,3 Front #2
Measles	- Front #1,2 Back #1,2
Meningitis	- Head #2,3 work down spine
Menopause	- Head #2 Front #4 Back #4
Migraine	- Head #1,2,3 Back #3
Morning Sickness	- Head #2,3 Front #2,3
Motion Sickness	- Head #2,3
Multiple Sclerosis	- Head #1,2,3 Front #1
Nausea	- Head #3 Front #2,3
Nightmares	- Head #1
Obesity	- Head #1,2,3,4
Osteoporosis	- Head #4 Back #3
Panic Attacks	- Head #3 Front #1,3 Back #3
Parkinson's Disease	- Head #1,2,3
Pneumonia	- Front #1,2 Back #2 sides
Prostate	- Front #4 Back #4
Psoriasis	- Head #2,3 Front #1 Back #3
Radiation	- Head #2 Front #1,3 Back #3
Sciatica	- Back #4
Scoliosis	- Back #1
Shingles	- Head #2,3 Back #1
Shock	- Head #2,3 Front #1 Back #3
Speech Problems	- Head #2,3,4
Spondylosis	- Back #1
Stress	- Front #2 Back #3
Stroke	- Head #1,2,3,4
Throat Problems	- Head #4
Tonsillitis	- Head #1 Front #1
TMJ	- Back #1 hands in front of ears
Urinary Tract Infection	- Front #4

Head Position 1

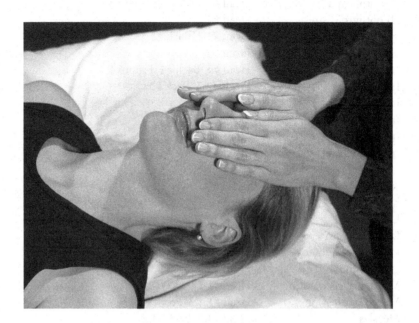

Head Position 2

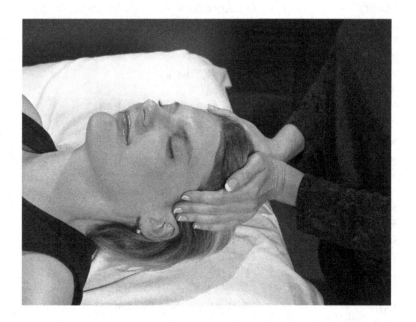

Head Position 3

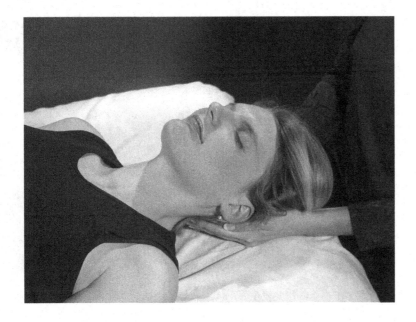

Head Position 4

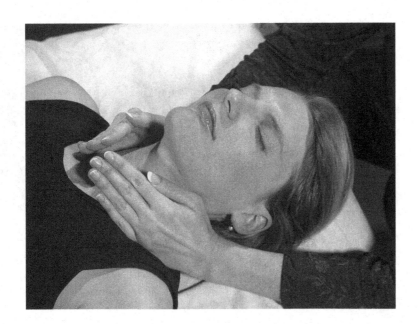

Front Position 1

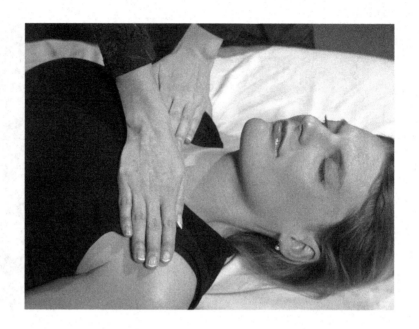

Front Position 2

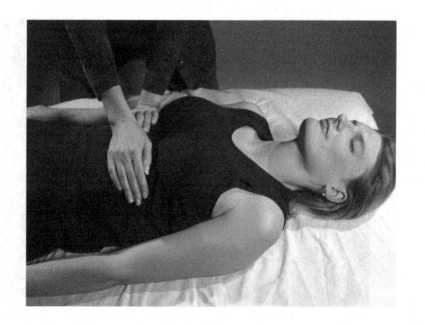

Front Position 3

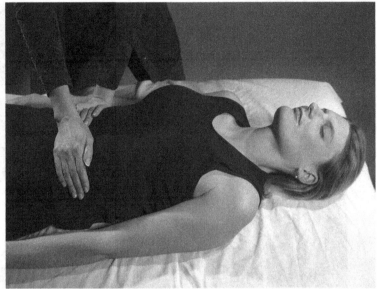

Front Position 4

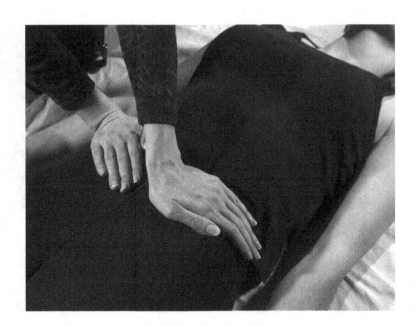

Back Position 1

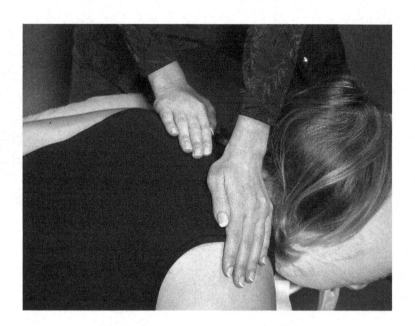

Back Position 2

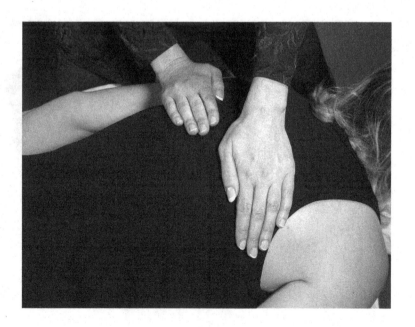

Back Position 3

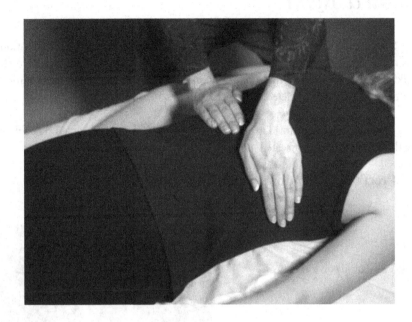

Back Position 4

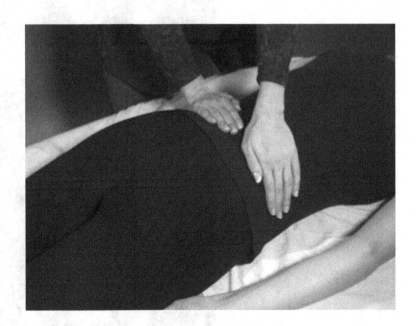

Chapter 9
Seated Reiki

Seated Reiki can be offered at Reiki shares, school fairs, conferences, conventions, or businesses. It is perfect to use when there is no room for a table and time is a factor. Seated Reiki takes less time than a traditional session because the hand positions are combined. Seated Reiki may be completed in 15 to 20 minutes.

The receiver sits comfortably in a low back chair, with legs uncrossed. The following are the hand positions for seated Reiki:

Practitioner standing behind the receiver:

∾ Hands on top of head

∾ Hands on shoulders

Practitioner standing beside the receiver:

∾ Hands on forehead and base of skull

∾ Hands on chest and upper back

∾ Hands on abdomen and sacrum (if it can be reached)

Practitioner standing in front of the receiver:

∾ Hands on knees

∾ Hands on top of feet

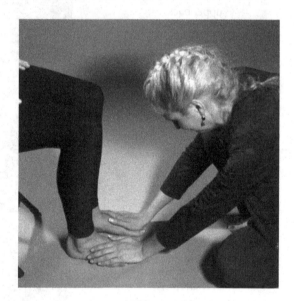

Chapter 10
Practicing Reiki

Scanning with Reiki

Scanning is used as an assessment tool at the beginning of a session, or a smoothing tool at the end of a session. Scanning is done by holding the hands about two inches above the body. Beginning at the head, slowly move both hands down over the front of the body toward the feet. You want to be aware of changes in the energy field. The energy may feel different to each person. Your hands may feel heat, cold, tingling, pressure or heaviness. All are legitimate feelings. Be aware of changes. Locations over the body where you feel energy changes are places to concentrate on during the Reiki healing session.

At the end of a session, you may scan the body again with your hands to make sure the energy feels smooth and calm.

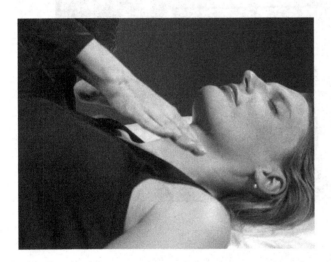

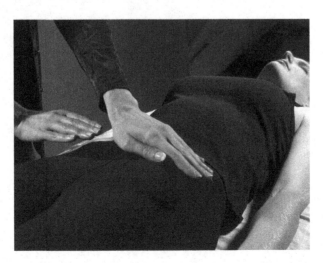

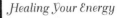

Beaming Reiki

Beaming is sending Reiki to a place or person that you cannot physically touch. You can beam Reiki energy across the room when you cannot touch a person with burns. You can beam Reiki energy to a rabid squirrel. I beamed Reiki energy to victims of a car accident right after it happened. I arrived before the ambulance. I also beam Reiki to the TV every time a football player gets injured during a game.

Beaming is done simply by bringing the hands up, palms facing away, and thinking about sending Reiki energy to a situation. I always send Reiki and bless everyone after I pass an automobile accident.

Reiki and Animals

Animals love Reiki. You may notice animals are more attracted to you after your attunement to Reiki energy. Distant Reiki can be sent to animals in the wild when they are acting strangely and cannot be touched.

Pets in the home enjoy receiving Reiki anytime. My cat will lie on my lap for an hour to receive Reiki. Animals cannot receive too much Reiki because when they have had enough, they will get up and move. Some small animals may only take a few minutes of Reiki in the beginning.

Reiki in Hospitals

In 2007, the USA Today, reported that over 800 hospitals in the United States are using Reiki. Many states have begun using volunteer Reiki Practitioners in hospitals. It is especially requested before and after surgery and on the oncology/cancer units. Thousands of nurses have been trained in Reiki. However, they do not always have the time to perform Reiki while on duty. Volunteers fill that gap. They provide Reiki for patients, families and staff. Some hospitals have requirements such as being Reiki second degree, and most require that providers carry insurance. Hospitals currently using Reiki volunteers are located in Maine, New Hampshire, Massachusetts, Connecticut, Arizona, and California. Check with your local hospital to see if you can join or start a volunteer Reiki Program in your area.

Research in hospitals have shown positive outcomes. After receiving a Reiki session, a majority report relaxation, sleepiness, decreased stress and decreased pain levels. More research is underway at the University of Michigan which is studying the use of Reiki as a treatment for neuropathy from diabetes. The National Institutes of Health's National Center for Complementary and Alternative Medicine is also sponsoring research studies on Reiki's effect on blood glucose levels, AIDS, fibromyalgia and prostate cancer.

In southern Maine, all five hospitals now offer Reiki treatments to patients. The volunteer coordinator sets up the time for the Reiki practitioner. The Reiki session is provided in the patient's room and many only last thirty minutes long, depending on the patient's diagnosis. I know patients who have received Reiki healing during their hospital stay, and found it relaxing and helpful.

As a nurse, I use Reiki on my patients immediately after surgery to speed healing of incisions. Reiki also provides pain relief for my clients experiencing acute or chronic pain. My clients remark that my hands are warm and the treatment feels relaxing.

Licensing Reiki

Licensing regulations for Reiki vary from state to state and from city to city. In Maine, there are no state regulations governing who can hang up a Reiki Practitioner sign, practice on people and charge money. However, in some cities in Maine, you may need to acquire a business license to practice Reiki. In other states, like Florida, the regulations now say that in order to practice hands-on Reiki, you must also be a licensed massage therapist. That law was passed by the Florida Board of Massage Therapy in 1999. They decided Reiki is massage because the treatment involves touching the body.

Whenever you practice, if you are placing your hands on a client, it is your responsibility to obtain liability insurance in case a client claims you injured her. The American Massage Therapy Association (AMTA) provides its professional members with liability insurance which covers Reiki and massage. It is also the practitioner's responsibility to obtain the city and state regulations where he or she lives to avoid practicing without a license. The laws are changing every day. As healthcare professionals, we need to be aware of and accountable to the laws and regulations in our area.

Client Information for Reiki

Name _____ Date _____

Address _____

City _____ State _____ Zip _____

Phone # (Home) _____ (Work) _____ (Cell) _____

Email _____ Date of Birth _____

Name of Spouse/Partner _____ Referred by _____

Occupation _____ Employer _____

Please check the following conditions that you are experiencing or have experienced:

_____ Cancer   _____ Diabetes
_____ High/Low Blood Pressure   _____ Currently Pregnant
_____ Heart Disease   _____ Allergies
_____ Seizures   _____ Migraines

Have you ever experienced a Reiki session before? _____

Where in your body do you feel you hold stress and tension?

Describe any pain you may have:

I, the Reiki practitioner, will keep all of this information confidential unless a release is signed by the client.

I understand that Reiki energy is for stress reduction and relaxation and is not a substitute for medical examinations or treatments. I understand that the Reiki practitioner does not diagnose illness or disease, and does not prescribe medical treatments or medications.

Client Signature _____ Date _____

Reiki Documentation Notes

Client Name: _____ Date: _____

Subjective: _____
_____

Objective: _____
_____

Assessment: _____
_____

Chakras
cleared: _____

Plan: _____
_____

Reiki Practitioner's Signature: _____

Client Name: _____ Date: _____

Subjective: _____
_____

Objective: _____
_____

Assessment: _____
_____

Chakras
cleared: _____

Plan: _____
_____

Reiki Practitioner's Signature: _____

SECTION IV   - ENERGY ENHANCERS

Chapter 11

Releasing Another's Energy

People naturally attract other people's energy. Translate energy into emotions and you will recognize yourself in this list. If you are holding on to the energy of your parents who treated you badly, an ex-partner who broke your heart, or an ill client you became too close too, then it is common to remember these memories with strong emotions. Those emotions are energy which stays trapped in our physical bodies until released. If the energy is not released, then ten years later can feel like yesterday and bring tears to your eyes. Unresolved emotions, such as grief and anger, can deplete energy which may lead to physical or emotional pain or illness. The good news is that it is never too late to start releasing old energy. And the better you are at letting go of ancient energy, the more efficient you can become at recognizing and releasing energy in the present.

When I first became a Reiki practitioner, I did not recognize the strength of other people's energy. As a community health nurse, I visited patients in their homes. One patient was experiencing an excruciating headache due to a brain tumor. I knew I could help, so I put my hands on his head. Within a few minutes his headache had lessened. I left, but before I could reach my next patient, I felt a terrible headache. This was odd to me. I never experience headaches. The pain became more severe. About an hour later, I realized it was not my headache. I intended to release this patient's energy. Within minutes my headache was completely gone. This was the beginning of many energy lessons I would learn.

As healthcare professionals caring for client's bodies, we are more prone to picking up their energy because we are directly in their energy field. We are assisting people with illness and physical or emotional overload. Illnesses and dis-eases by definition are unbalanced energy. The energy which is released needs to transfer some place. The healthcare practitioner does not intend to pick up unhealthy energy, but she is a prime suspect. The goal is to recognize when you are engaged in your clients energy field and have attracted their negative or exhausting energy. Then you can begin to release their energy.

The more you practice energy work, the more sensitive your hands become to energy. Your body is made to function with a certain amount of energy. The body cannot function in a healthy way if it is holding on to the energy of another being. Instead, excess energy creates an imbalance in the body's energy system. As you are helping treat your client's physical pain, their unbalanced energy may affect your energy. There are methods to release someone else's energy and keep your energy clear. The following is a list of techniques to help you stay grounded and release your client's energy. I have compiled this list from many practitioners and therapists I have known over the years. This list is divided into three categories.

Techniques to Release Energy

While providing direct client care:

- ෨ Shake or flick hands – Some therapists state that they do not feel the need to release the client's energy when working on them. However, I and others notice a feeling of tingling or heaviness in our hands as we are clearing energy and instinctively shake our hands or flick our fingers during a session.

- ෨ Imagine the person's energy going through your body, out your feet, into the ground.

- ෨ Imagine the excess energy being released into a bubble or balloon and floating away in the sky.

- ෨ Surround yourself with white healing light.

- ෨ Surround yourself with a clear, strong bubble.

- ෨ Yawn or exhale – You may find you feel the need to yawn or breathe deeply and blow off the exhale when you are releasing your client's energy or emotions. I sometimes tell my clients this so they do not think I am tired.

- ෨ Conscious release of energy – This is the technique I use every time I end a session. I have taught it to many clients and students. At the end of the session, place your hands wherever you were taught and feels right to you: feet, head, or abdomen. Any of these locations will work with intention because energy flows in and out of these areas. I place my hands on the top of the head and repeat three times to myself, "I have only my energy. I intend to release (client's name) energy". I feel my hands lift off their head when our energies have separated.

Practice this technique. Think of a client, or anyone's energy you are holding onto. Repeat this statement three times, aloud or silently. Remember to breathe. Notice the changes in your body.

"I have only my energy. I intend to release (*person's name*) energy."

Between clients:

- Wash hands in cold water – Always wash your hands after touching a client for infection control. Using cold water is better for cleaning energy from your hands.

- Wiping energy off arms – Using one hand, swipe down the other arm, stroking shoulder to hand, then switch arms.

- Burning sage – The Native Americans use sage to clear negative energy. White sage is the best. It can be bought as a smudge stick or single pieces. When clients have a lot of emotional release, I burn white sage before the next client arrives. Burn the sage, then blow it out and spread the smell around the room and over the massage table or chair.

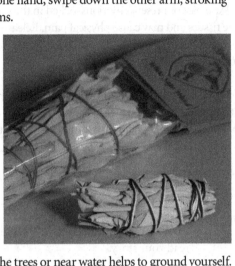

- Walk outside – Walking among the trees or near water helps to ground yourself.

- Take a nap – I know a therapist who always took a ten minute nap between clients to ground herself. Remember to set an alarm.

- Pray – Intend to ask a higher power to clear your space or yourself.

- Make noise – Drum or chant, say a mantra, exhale "Om".

- Blow out and relight candles – Each client receives new energy for their session.

- Move – dance around the table, or practice T'ai Chi Ch'uan.

- Drink plenty of water. (Twice your weight in ounces every day)

- Try a quick meditation or at least five deep breaths.

Every day:

- Walking, especially outside
- Exercise, free-style dance or movement
- Meditation
- Relaxation breathing
- Yoga
- Self healing with Reiki
- Polarity
- T'ai Chi Ch'uan
- Bioenergetic Movement
- Massage
- Gardening

Journaling

Releasing another's energy is easier if practiced on a daily basis. Over time, other people's energy permeates our energy field and is harder to disconnect from the past. Journaling is a process which allows old emotions to be released. It is a technique used to release past or present emotions locked in the body. Over time, those emotions store up in the tissues and may cause physical pain. Releasing these emotions gives you more energy to deal with daily situations. Research has proven a decrease in physical pain by the following journaling exercise.

A study published in the *Journal of the American Medical Association, April 14, 1999,* stated that people with asthma and rheumatoid arthritis significantly decrease their physical pain after writing 20 minutes a day for three consecutive days about a stressful event in their life.

Try this Exercise

Practice this writing exercise:

1. Choose a significant stressful event in your life. Remember, no one else has to read your story.

2. Write in a place where you will not be disturbed. You may write with pen and paper, or type.

3. Write for 20 minutes nonstop about the event, for three consecutive days.

4. Do not worry about spelling or grammar. The goal is to let the emotion out of your body.

5. Notice the changes in your body and attitude toward the event after each writing session, and again after the three days.

6. If you are so inclined, share your story with a friend or counselor.

7. You may destroy the writing by having a ceremony and tearing up the paper, or burning it in a safe place. Intend to release this event, energy, and emotion from your body.

Chapter 12
Writing Affirmations

I began reading Louise Hay's *You Can Heal Your Life* in the 1980's. Her book inspired my journey of using and believing in affirmations. I teach every client about affirmations and how our thoughts create energy and make our reality.

Affirmations are positive statements about the present. An affirmation may not be true when you start saying it, but puts the seed thought into the brain. The brain cannot tell the difference between reality and non-reality. Use affirmations as goals you wish to accomplish, but act as if they have already happened.

Techniques to write affirmation goals:

1. Always write in the present tense.
2. Be specific about the words you choose.
3. Use the words "I, we, or your name" in every goal.
4. Avoid using the words "try, will, not, never, should, would, could, or want". You can use "choose".
5. Include a deadline date if applicable.

Examples of affirmations:

I attract ten new clients within six months.

I love my body and trust its wisdom.

I have joy.

My life is perfectly balanced.

I live a fulfilled healthy life every day.

I love myself.

Affirmations for healing (say three times):

"I intend to release (person's name) energy."

"I am a clear energy channel."

"I have only my energy."

"I hear and trust my intuition."

Fill in your affirmations:

I love…

I earn…

My career…

My life…

My relationship…

I choose…

Write more affirmations for other specific areas of your life:

1. _____
   _____
   _____
   _____

2. _____
   _____
   _____
   _____

3. _____
   _____
   _____
   _____

4. _____
   _____
   _____
   _____

Techniques for using your affirmations:

1. Write down your affirmations.
2. Rewrite your affirmations daily.
3. State or read your affirmations daily.
4. Place your affirmations on sticky notes around your house, car or office where you will see them daily.
5. Take deep breaths while speaking your affirmations.
6. Release your affirmations into the universe.

Taking Care of Yourself

How balanced is your life and how well are you taking care of yourself? How much energy you have to share with others depends upon how much energy you acquire.

For each statement, answer and give yourself points:

Do 7 days a week – 5 points

Do 5 days a week – 3 points

Do 2 to 3 days a week – 2 points

Never do – 0 points

1. _____ I get 7 to 8 hours of sleep.
2. _____ I give and receive safe touch and affection.
3. _____ I have 20 minutes of quiet time or time by myself.
4. _____ I see or talk to friends or relatives.
5. _____ I see the positive side of a situation.
6. _____ I avoid cigarettes.
7. _____ I limit my alcoholic beverages to two.
8. _____ I am able to pay my bills.
9. _____ I pray or meditate.
10. _____ I drink at least 64 ounces of water.
11. _____ I drink less than 20 ounces of caffeine.
12. _____ I stretch or exercise for 30 minutes.
13. _____ I laugh daily.
14. _____ I enjoy my work or career.
15. _____ I have time to do what I want.
16. _____ I take multiple vitamin supplements.
17. _____ I take multiple mineral supplements.
18. _____ I eat breakfast.
19. _____ I limit my white sugar/candy intake.
20. _____ I take only necessary prescription medications.

_____ Total Score

Perfect score = 100 Amazing! My hat is off to you.

Goal score = 80 Excellent! You are listening to your body and have enough energy to live in the present and be healthy every day.

Passing score = 60 Congratulations! You are taking care of yourself daily.

Under 60 = It might be helpful to pick some specific categories to focus on to decrease your stress. Use the answers of 0 or 2 points to say as your daily affirmations.

Chapter 13
Visualizing Your Future

Describe your perfect life. What would you be doing? Where would you be working? Who would you be with? If you do not know the answers to these questions, you cannot get there. It is not about having a plan, it is about having a goal. What is your dream, your big wish?

Visualization is a technique used by many to achieve their reality. By creating your universe the way you want it and living as if it has already happened, you create your future. Many athletes use visualization or imagery to help them focus. Tiger Woods "sees" the golf ball fall in the hole. Michael Jordan imagined the basketball swish through the hoop. Those are very easy, literal examples.

Visualization can be used in every area of your life, relationships, career, money, health, and education. Always remember, be careful what you ask for, you may just get it. It is important to be specific, but you have to let go of the end result. Be specific about every part of what you want. If you are visualizing your perfect job, be precise and write down the hours you want to work, amount of pay, location, what you want your office to look like, job description, anything you can think of. If it is a person, describe their hair color, height, weight, nationality, hobbies, values, personality and the kind of relationship you want to have with them. Trust me, if you forget something, the universe will surprise you. The universe has a wonderful sense of humor. You will get what you want and more. But remember, the universe does not understand time.

When visualizing our future, the problem does not come with asking for what we want. The problem is our expectation of what that outcome will look like and when it will happen. The universe may respond very quickly on some topics, within a month or two, or longer on others, if there is something you need to learn first. Writing a list of very specific descriptions is the first step in knowing what you want. By putting it on paper, you are actually creating it. Thought put into action as intention is taken very seriously by the universe. It does not ask if you are ready, it will give you what you want or think you want. Sometimes when you get what you want or ask for, you realize that it is not really what you wanted after all.

The process of using words and pen, paper or computer is one way to tell the universe what you want. Another way is to make a collage. Make sure you have at least an hour or more to be alone to focus on your collage. Using a big sheet of poster paper, scissors and old magazines, cut out words and pictures you like. Paste them any way you want on the paper. When I design collages, I like to date them too. I have created many wonderful collages and opportunities in my life.

The more senses you use to visualize your goals, the stronger the action becomes. You can put your collage where you see it every day. If you are visualizing a house or car, you can carry a picture of it with you. Imagine how you feel when you have accomplished this goal.

Once you learn how to create, visualize, and manifest what you want and desire, you might notice that it really does work. However, Shakti Gawain, in her book *Creative Visualization,* discusses that once you acquire the material items you desire, maybe you will find that they are not what you really want. I manifest lessons in my life. For myself, along with the material object, comes an opportunity to learn. I invite you to decide what you would like to manifest in your life and be open to the possibilities you might receive.

Visualization can be used in every area of your life: relationships, career, money, health, and education. Always remember, be careful what you ask for, you may just get it.

Start with your life goals:

Where do you choose to be in six months?

One year?

Five years?

Use those goals to help create your focus for your visualization.

What do you want to change: career, relationship, finances, health, or education?

Remember, if you only focus on one area, are you willing to give up the other areas in your life to achieve what you believe you want? (Do you want your career if you lose your marriage or health?) Be realistic – don't work on all your goals at once.

Describe your perfect life.

Be specific.

Think of every detail.

How do you feel it? The more senses you use, the better.

Write it down. Use pen and paper or computer.

Make a collage: Using words is one way to tell the universe what you want. Another way is to make a collage. Make sure you have at least an hour or more to be alone to focus on your collage. Using a big sheet of poster paper, scissors and old magazines, cut out words and pictures you like. Paste them any way you want on the paper. It is helpful to date the collage, too.

Let it go: Visualize your perfect life and release what you think it will look like when it shows up. Expect the unexpected.

Trust the Universe: Trust that you are exactly where you are supposed to be.

Appendix
Suggested Music for Relaxation, Meditation and Reiki Sessions

Over the years I have listened to many CD's while giving and receiving energy and bodywork sessions. Listed below are my favorites. This music brings me to a place of peace and knowing that we are all connected by energy.

They all have a different sound. Find the one that resonates with you.

Chant
> *"Benedictine Monks"*, Angel Records, 1994

Steven Halpern
> www.stevenhalpern.com,   www.innerpeacemusic.com
> Open Channel Sound Company, San Anselmo, CA
> *"Higher Ground"*, 1992
> *"Sound Healing"*, 1999
> *"Music for Massage"*, 2000
> *"Chakra Suite"*, 2003

Lifescapes (Available at Target stores)
> *"Sleep"*, Compass Productions, 2001
> *"Meditations: Native American Flute"*, Compass Productions, 2000

Andreas Mock of Merlin's Magic
> *"Light Reiki Touch"*, Inner Worlds Music, Boulder, CO, 1995

R. Carlos Nakai
> *"Mythic Dreamer: Native American Flute"*, Canyon Records, Phoenix, AZ, 1998
> *"Canyon Trilogy"* , Canyon Records, Phoenix, AZ, 2003

Hilary Stagg
> *"The Edge of Forever"*, Real Music, Sausalito, CA, 1993

Chuck Wild
> *"Liquid Mind IV: Unity"*, Chuck Wild Records, Hollywood, CA, 2000
> *"Liquid Mind V: Serenity"*, Chuck Wild Records, Hollywood, CA, 2001

References for Reiki

A Complete Book of Reiki Healing,
Brigitte Muller & Horst H. Gunther, Life Rhythm, 1995

"An Introduction to Reiki",
National Center for Complementary and Alternative Medicine,
April 24, 2006, http://nccam.nih.gov/health/reiki

"Ancient Wisdom, Modern Care",
Meredith Kendall, MSN, RN, Advance for Nurses, March 26, 2007,
pp 13, 24

Essential Reiki: A Complete Guide to an Ancient Healing Art,
Diane Stein, The Crossing Press Inc., Freedom, CA, 1995

Practical Reiki,
Richard Ellis, Sterling Publishing Co., Inc., New York, 1999

"Reiki",
Clare Horn, Natural Health, September 1999, p 41

Reiki: Universal Life Energy,
Bodo J. Baginski & Shalila Sharamon, Life Rhythm, 1988

Reiki: The Healing Touch,
William Lee Rand, Vision Publications, 1991, www.reiki.org

Reiki Master Manual,
William Lee Rand, Vision Publications, 2003

The Power of Reiki: An Ancient Hands-on Healing Technique,
Tanmaya Honervogt, Reiki Master, An Owl Book, Henry Holt, NY, 1998

The Reiki Handbook,
Larry Arnold & Sandy Nevius, PSI Press, Harrisburg, PA, 1982

The Spirit of Reiki,
Walter Lubeck, Frank Arjava Petter, William Lee Rand, Lotus Press, 2001

References for the Chakras

Chakra Balancing,
    Anodea Judith, Boulder, CO, 2003, www.sacredcenters.com

Chakra Clearing,
    Doreen Virtue, Ph.D., Hay House Inc., Carlsbad, CA, 1998

"Chakra Yoga: Journey to Wholeness",
    Todd Norian, Kripalu Institute, 1998

Energy Medicine,
    Donna Eden, Penguin Putnam Inc., NY, 1998

Hands of Light: A Guide to Healing Through the Human Energy Field,
    Barbara Ann Brennan, Bantam Books, 1987

The Book of Chakras,
    Ambika Wauters, Barrons, NY, 2002

"The Energetics of Healing",
    Caroline Myss, video, Sounds True, Boulder, Co, 1997

The Polarity Workbook,
    Nancy Anna Risley, Polarity Realization Center, Ipswich, MA, 1991

*The Sevenfold Journey: Reclaiming Mind, Body & Spirit Through the
    Chakras,*
    Anodea Judith & Selene Vega, The Crossing Press, Freedom, CA,
    1995

Wheels of Light,
    Rosalyn Bruyere, Fireside, New York, NY, 1994

References for Healing and Human Energy

Awakening Intuition,
> Mona Lisa Schulz, Three Rivers Press, New York, NY, 1998

Business Mastery,
> Cheri Sohnen-Moe, Sohnen-Moe Associates, Inc., Tucson, AZ, 1991

Creative Visualization: Use the Power of Your Imagination to Create What You Want in Your Life,
> Shakti Gawain, Natarai Publishing, Novato, CA, 1995

"Energy Therapies and Diabetes Mellitus",
> Diane W. Guthrie, PhD and Maureen Gamble, BSN, MA,
> Diabetes Spectrum 14:149-153, 2001

Heal Your Body,
> Louise Hay, Hay House Inc., Carson, CA, 1988

Positive Energy,
> Judith Orloff, M.D., Three Rivers Press, New York, NY, 2004

Reference Guide for Essential Oils,
> Connie and Alan Higley, Abundant Health, Spanish Fork, UT, 2014

You Can Heal Your Life,
> Louise Hay, Hay House Inc., Carson, CA, 1984

Why People Don't Heal and How They Can,
> Caroline Myss, Three Rivers Press, New York, NY, 1997

About the Author:

Marie King Hardman, a dedicated healthcare professional, assists people in their healing process. She believes physical pain is experienced if unbalanced energy or emotional pain has not yet found an outlet for release. Her approach to healing, bodywork and teaching provides that outlet. Her belief in the connection between the physical and energetic bodies, and illness and health, shows in her passion for teaching holistic health.

Marie began this journey in 1994 and has nationally taught chakra and massage courses. Marie is a Registered Nurse, Licensed Massage Therapist, and Reiki Master Teacher. She has earned a Bachelor's Degree in Nursing, a Master's Degree in Adult Education and a Master's Degree in Nursing Education.

Printed in the United States
By Bookmasters